A
Child
Called
Noah

A
CHILD CALLED

NOAH

A FAMILY JOURNEY

Josh Greenfeld

A Harvest/HBJ Book
HARCOURT BRACE JOVANOVICH, PUBLISHERS
San Diego   New York   London

Requests for permission to make copies of
any part of the work should be mailed to:
Trade Permissions, Henry Holt and Company, Inc.,
115 West 18th Street, New York, New York 10011.

Published by arrangement
with Henry Holt and Company, Inc.
A portion of this work appeared in *Life* magazine.

Library of Congress Cataloging-in-Publication Data

Greenfeld, Josh.
    A child called Noah: a family journey/Josh Greenfeld.
      p. cm.
    "A Harvest/HBJ book."
    ISBN 0-15-616862-6 (pbk.)
    1. Greenfeld, Noah Jiro, 1966-
    2. Brain-damaged children—United States—Biography.
    3. Brain-damaged children—United States—Family relationships.
    4. Greenfeld, Noah Jiro, 1966-
    I. Title.
    [RJ496.B7G72 1988]
    362.3—dc 19
    [B]   88-17734

Printed in the United States of America

First Harvest/HBJ edition

A B C D E

for "our children,"
for their parents

Karl Taro Greenfeld
born November 26, 1964 in Kobe, Japan
of confused parentage
(Mr. and Mrs. Josh Greenfeld)
ambivalently announces
the birth of a sibling
Noah Jiro Greenfeld
on July 1, 1966 in North Tarrytown, New York

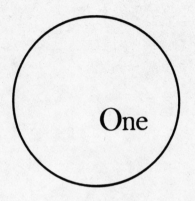

One

July, 1970

The balding father pushes the shopping cart down the su-permarket aisle, his four-year-old son sitting on the shelf within, sneakered feet dangling through the wire rungs. A fat and friendly woman stops and smiles at the boy. "You're beautiful," she says, bending over him. "He's beautiful."

"Thank you," says the father.

"What's your name?" she asks the boy. He turns his head away, making some unintelligible sounds. "What's your name?" she asks again. The boy begins to rock back and forth in the shopping cart. "Don't be shy," the woman continues. "Can't you tell me your name?"

"No," says the father, "he can't."

The woman looks up with sudden concern. "Doesn't he talk?"

"Not anymore," says the father.

"I'm sorry," says the woman, gently reaching out to pat the boy, who ducks his head away.

"What's the matter with him? He's so beautiful."

"We don't know," replies the father.

"Oh"—the woman recovers her natural joviality—"don't worry. Whatever is bothering him, he'll grow out of it, I'm sure."

I wish I could be sure. The boy is my son Noah.

At the age of four Noah is neither toilet-trained nor does he feed himself. He seldom speaks expressively, rarely employs his less-than-a-dozen-word vocabulary. His attention span in a new toy is a matter of split seconds, television engages him for only an odd moment occasionally, he is never interested in other children for very long. His main activities are lint-catching, thread-pulling, blanket-sucking, spontaneous giggling, inexplicable crying, eye-squinting, wall-hugging, circle-walking, bed-bouncing, jumping, rocking, door-closing, and incoherent babbling addressed to his finger-flexing right hand. But two years ago Noah spoke in complete sentences, had a vocabulary of well over 150 words, sang the verses of his favorite songs, identified the objects and animals in his picture books, was all but toilet-trained, and practically ate by himself.

What's the matter with Noah? For the longest time it seemed to depend upon what diagnosis we were willing to shop around for. We'd been told he was mentally retarded; emotionally disturbed; autistic; schizophrenic; possibly brain-damaged; or that he was suffering from a Chinese-box combination of these conditions. But we finally discovered that the diagnosis didn't seem to matter; it was all so sadly academic. The medical profession was merely playing Aristotelian nomenclature and classification games at our expense. For though we live in one of the richest states in the nation, there was no single viable treatment immediately available for Noah, no matter what category he could eventually be assigned to.

On a statistical level, Noah, of course, is just an actuarial speck or a genetic smudge. It is estimated that there are almost ten million mentally—or emotionally—ill children in America, over two million of these are seriously disturbed; in addition, there are over two million mentally retarded children, and these figures do not include the palsied or the epileptic, those children suffering only motor impairments. The odds on the next baby born in this country being or becoming severely retarded or seriously disturbed are about 33 in 1,000.

And not the least victims of this common but rarely foreseen malady will be the child's parents and family. They may delight at first in the tranquil docility or uncommon beauty of their child. For schizophrenic children are very often—and autistic children are invariably—beautiful, as if their untouchable imperviousness to the usual course of human events keeps them so. Then, however, there will be months and years of anguish, roller-coaster cycles of elation and depression as the parents try to deny the evidence before their eyes that their child is less than ordinary or normal, is indeed "exceptional," to use one of the medical euphemisms. In addition, parents will find themselves getting little in the way of help and much in the way of confusion from the medical profession. Most neurologists, they will discover, would rather describe than prescribe; most psychiatrists are more apt to make the parents feel guilty than to suggest a program to help the child. After a while the local pediatrician himself may begin to regard both child and parents as troublemakers and deviants, out to disrupt his rounds of runny noses and infected ears.

Yet perhaps the best way for me to tell what it's been like for Noah—and for us as a family—is not as the professional writer I am, trained to carefully and abstractly plot ahead, but as the amateur parent I also am, thoroughly confused and beleaguered every step of the way. Let me cull some entries from my journal, for though often muddled and uninformed, I think they can best communicate who we are as people, and the nature and quality of the experience.

July 1, 1966

I'm a father. I'm drunk. I have another son. His name is Noah Jiro. He was born this evening a few minutes after seven and weighed seven pounds, ten ounces. And whereas Karl seemed to look like me at birth, Noah is luckier. He looks like his Japanese mother, Foumi.

I saw Noah Jiro as he passed on the way to the maternity ward. And next I saw Foumi. She was not very sleepy. Though induced at full term, it was supposed to be a natural childbirth, so I guess she had had only a pinch of anesthesia when it came time to sew her up. I followed the caravan. And soon I was standing at the nursery window, noting proudly to the stranger next to me how much hair Noah had.

I think of my dead father now. I think of the living

Noah I already love. He seems like the son of my father to me, just as Karl is the son of my mother. I do not know why, but that is so. Of course, they are both the sons of Foumi too. But then nothing so important is ever that simple.

Anyway, I am happier than I ever thought I would be. I wanted a daughter, I know. But I rejoice in having a second son. Noah Jiro—the name is a breath of hope.

July 2, 1966

I am not such a good daddy. I am not used to the full-time chore of baby-tending. I was a bit careless. I left Karl alone for a moment this afternoon when I went downstairs to put the laundry in the washing machine. I returned to find a broken glass on the floor, its shards splintered in many directions. Luckily Karl was not hurt.

I saw Noah in the hospital today. He seemed to look just the way Karl had looked during his first days of life. Suddenly, in a small but overwhelming way time stood still.

What the hell am I doing in Westchester with two baby sons? How did I get here? I lived in Greenwich Village for ten years, from 1950 to 1960. All during that time I viewed the Village as a casual company in an army, "repple depple"—replacement center. I never felt permanence, I always sensed transiency. Sometimes I would even fantasize an army-style reveille: "All of Jones Street, Cornelia Street, Leroy Street, Morton Street—fall out in front of your billets!"

There is duty call, roster assignments: "Smith—another year at Louis's. Coombs—six more months at the White Horse. Rosenblatt—back to Columbia to get a graduate degree. Horowitz—sit around the Rienzi for one more year. Kane—transferred from the New School to a job with computers in Louisville. Harrison—an uptown gig in advertising. Miss Samuels—marriage to that doctor in the Bronx. Miss Carlson—home to Minnesota. Miss Evans—out of Stella Adler's acting classes and into the Omaha Community Theatre. Miss Shafransky—a nervous breakdown: six months at Rockland State. Mr. Adler—upon the completion of your analysis proceed TDY to Ypsilanti, Michigan, to work in their clinical psychology program."

The rest of us fall out. Lovers, friends, analysts, and patients bidding each other sad farewells: "Don't worry, I'll write to you from my new outfit." But one knew they never would.

And, indeed, I had several TDY—temporary duty —assignments—one to the army itself, summers in Provincetown, Fire Island, and Amagansett, an extended trip to Europe, a brief junket to Cuba—before I received my permanent assignment.

In the spring of 1960 after getting a Guggenheim which I intended to squander in France, I went to the MacDowall Colony, an artists' retreat in Peterborough, New Hampshire. I planned to stay there until July 15. I stayed longer. I met a painter, Foumiko Kometani. The bureaucracy of the Department of Immigration encouraged the reality of a quick marriage rather than the romance of a lingering affair. And instead of going to France or returning to the Village—what with European boat fares and Village rents—Foumi and I spent the next two years in Brooklyn Heights getting up a stake. A play of mine was done off-Broadway, I taught at NYU and Pace, I wrote magazine articles, I reviewed books for a news magazine. Foumi worked for an insurance company, for NYU at registration time. In 1962 we were able to make a getaway. And we decided to get away to Japan. At least, I decided to. I thought: I could never understand my wife, in which ways she was an individual and in which ways she was a type, how a specific and how a generic, unless I did so.

But Foumi wanted to go to Europe. She'd never been there. So we compromised. We decided to go to Japan by way of Europe. We further agreed, as a literal ground rule, not to fly.

So we traveled the wet ways and the railways through Holland, Belgium, France, Spain, Italy, Greece, Egypt, India, Ceylon, Vietnam, Singapore, Hong Kong, to Japan. We had planned to stay in Japan for a year; we stayed there for two and a half years. And then we decided to return to America. But not as we had left. Now we had a baby: Karl Taro.

And I did not want to have to plop down in a hotel with a baby. I wrote to some friends in New York asking if they knew of any apartments or houses available for rental. And a publisher friend told me of a half of a house on a hill, which we rented blind. In Westchester.

Over all the beers I guzzled at the Remo and the Kettle of Fish and Johnny Romero's and the Riv and the White Horse and the Cedar Street Bar and Gilhooleys; over all the cups of coffee I sipped at the Figaro and Rienzi and Limelight and the Lion's Head; over all the martinis I nursed at the Waverly Lounge and the Jumble Shop and the Dickens Room; over all the red wine I drank at Felini's and Mary's; and during all the nights of prowling down all the elephant paths of the village and the long days of numb sun sitting on the concrete lip of the "snake pit" in the center of the park and walking down its spoke-like bypaths grimly searching joyous companionship; and during all the meals at the Griddle and Chumleys and the Waldorf and even at the sausage stand at the end of Minetta Lane; during the countless morning-after breakfasts at Humpty Dumpty's and Howard Johnson's and Joe's; during all the years when 14th Street was my uptown Rubicon—I never dreamt that I would wind up a Westchester resident. A father. A family man with two sons.

July 4, 1966

I don't know what's worse: a first baby or a second baby, not quite knowing what you're in for or knowing exactly what demands the normal routine of baby care entails—but it is good to have a second son. It pleases the male vanity, it makes one feel the winds of luck fanning one's plumage. Noah Jiro Greenfeld is a reality. Karl Taro Greenfeld has a brother. I cannot imagine my sons bearing any other names.

These past few days—in addition to my twice-daily visits—I've phoned Foumi about ten times a day. And each time I feel she wants to talk to me long past the natural conclusion of our conversation. And I want to keep talking to her. We miss each other badly.

July 10, 1966

We're back at the basic training of baby raising. We sleep when we can in three-hour snatches, we wander about in perpetual states of fatigue. And now we have Karl to present psychological problems: he moans and whines all day long. Noah is comparatively easy—except for feedings; he seems to have a more phlegmatic personality than Karl had. While Karl looked strong and western and very masculine, Noah looks like a Bunraku puppet or a figure in one of those eighteenth-century woodprints; intensely fragile, extremely delicate. And he is genuinely attractive, a really beautiful baby. Both my sons fill me with kinds of love I never dreamt possible.

Dreamt . . . I dreamt last night of my father. I was sitting with him on the platform of a synagogue. He was being introduced. And the congregation cheered for him. I guess somewhere in my search to understand myself I am meeting him again.

July 11, 1966

Noah has become a part of our lives. He still wakes us at night, of course, but we sleep better afterward. And Foumi has been able to come down the stairs twice today.

July 12, 1966

Time has altered me remarkably. I grow a beard and I wear sandals, but I am bogged down with diapers and feedings, washing machines and dryers, and beginning next month I face the daily grind of commuting to New York. I've taken a job, ending my precarious free-lance writer existence. I've had to: a family makes a realist out of any man. I can skimp on meals; my two sons can't. I have dreams to sustain me, while they only live ferociously in the present. They must cry boisterously whenever they are denied, while I, of course, can merely shrug wistfully.

July 13, 1966

Foumi and I have been quarreling. Because we're worrying about Noah. He's vomited out his milk after every feeding lately.

July 16, 1966

We're having a heat wave, a New York heat wave. By two o'clock in the afternoon as the day wears on one begins to feel enclosed in warm, sticky gauze full of someone else's mucus. Especially if one did not sleep well the night before. And that happens to us most nights. Because of the baby. Because of Foumi's nursing techniques. Because of our fights about it. Foumi gives both the breast and the bottle, which means double time, double duty, and a wake-up period in the middle of the night that can last a full two hours. It did last night.

July 17, 1966

I had a lovely evening with Karl. We played, we rolled on the floor, we promenaded about the sun porch; he mimicked my every action. And then we went upstairs to see the baby. I picked him up and asked him to kiss Noah. And in spite of the obvious staged quality of the moment, Foumi and I looked at each other, blinked hard, and pressed hands tightly.

July 21, 1966

Noah seems to be becoming a person much quicker than Karl did. Perhaps it's because we're less apprehensive about him as a baby in every way. Foumi too seems to be recovering more rapidly after Noah's birth. Or is it all in my sweaty imagination?

July 26, 1966

I cannot deceive Karl. If I want to be with him, he knows it and squeals his delight. If I'm begrudging him the time, he shows it in moans and whelps. One good thing about working at home has been that I can spend so much time with him—and Noah; a bad thing about working at home has been that I waste so much time doing so. Noah looks friendlier than Karl did to me at the same age; his eyes seem gentler, softer, rather than full of wonder, but his body appears so fragile that sometimes I hesitate to pick him up and hug him tightly.

July 30, 1966

In preparation for the start of my job tomorrow, I had a haircut today, and when I returned home Karl didn't recognize me. He cried and cried. And now the baby's crying—or coughing. Foumi's in the tub. So I'll have to go to him. Noah Jiro tic-tock hic-coughs away my life.

August 23, 1966

Noah still does not sleep through the night—and so neither do we.

I took Noah, then Karl, into the bath with me. Karl is more fun each day, beginning to talk, saying "huh" and "hi," and having more and more a sense of what's going on. Noah, though, I think, is cuter—and more sensitive. Words I never thought of applying to Karl. Noah's also weak, not as strong as Karl. But perhaps it only seems that way, since each day I'm comparing him to a growing, hardening Karl.

Now Foumi wants to buy a house. It will be good for the family. It will be good for the boys. Sure. But if we get a house, then I'll be stuck with monthly payments forever. I'm not sure I want my job any longer. I'm not sure I want a house at all. I'm not sure what I want anymore. The freshness of return is gone, the clearness of perception vanished. I feel vaguely but helplessly trapped.

The job is easy. It's like high school, college, the army, the old neighborhood: an occasion rather than a function, a game more than a commitment. Only it's so debilitating, keeps me from doing the writing I want to do.

It rained, and the day was dreary and the train was late in getting home. But I walked in the door so glad to see Foumi, and my arms almost aching to hug Karl and pick up Noah. Story-book happy.

September 23, 1966

We've made a bid on a house, a new one, just being built, and I'm not sure whether I'm worried more about its being accepted or rejected.

September 25, 1966

The deal is set. The builder will give us a second mortgage and the bank will let us take over the builder's first mortgage. Now, the children in bed, Foumi sits across the table from me, calmly, elegantly peeling an orange, and I recall those quiet, creative evenings in Japan, those many years two children ago, and hope that in our new house I might again experience a rebirth, a thawing out, and a coming up for air of my own choosing.

October 1, 1966

The builder of the house we're buying has suddenly tacked on some extra charges. Woe's me. But there are joys: Karl is growing, using words, inventive at play, a boy in love with trucks and cars. Noah smiles continually. Paternity pats me warmly now.

But when I came home last night, sitting in the train, riding along the Hudson with my fellow commuters, the sky seemed full of tears and America a very sad place indeed. I still feel that. I want to return to Japan. But Foumi's right: if we have a house, then we can go away because we have a point of eventual return. Without a house we become but homeless wanderers.

October 8, 1966

Whenever I play with Noah, Karl looks at him with a look that reminds me of the way my older sister used to look at me—discomfiting hate tinged with shame, displeasure in an area that once richly promised great delight.

November 26, 1966

Today is Karl Taro's birthday—two years old—and we observed it by going to the doctor's for Noah's shots. Noah is so different from Karl. He's beautiful in a feminine way. He laughs at life before he cries at it. Indeed, last night he woke us up with his laughing.

November 28, 1966

Karl talks more and more, and Noah has become a little person. These are really the only important developments in my life. The rest is garbage. And now I'll take the family for a drive to look at our new house.

Our house will soon be ready, and we'll move into it in about two weeks. So I've decided to leave my job in three weeks. I look forward to living in the new house and working there and watching my kids grow up there. I don't look forward to paying all the bills, though. But it's worth the gamble.

December 15, 1966

We're in our house. The boys have adjusted to it immediately: Noah by just lying in his crib and smiling inscrutably, Karl by traipsing about everywhere inquisitively.

January 27, 1967

Earlier this morning Karl walked into my study; he wanted to play with my books. I let him do so for a while. Then I gently ushered him out. The look on his face: such deep disappointment, such utter betrayal. But writing at home, unfortunately, I have to be cruel to him as I discipline myself.

February 3, 1967

Yesterday I took Karl for his first train ride. We had walked down to the station when I realized that a train would be leaving soon and thought he might enjoy the idea of getting on one for a few minutes before it left the station. Once on the train a conductor pointed out the nonsmoker to me. But I said: "We just want to look over the train. My boy's never been on a train before." And then I asked the conductor if we could ride as far as the next stop. "Be my guest," he said. And Karl and I rode into the next station, Karl nervously quiet, his face pressed against the windowpane. Then we taxied home. I still can't quite figure out Karl's reaction. The whole deal left him quite nonplussed. I suppose he's got the makings of a commuter in him.

February 8, 1967

Foumi's feeling sick—or pregnant—or both. If she's pregnant, I think we'll go off to Japan for a twelve-dollar completely legal abortion. She just isn't up to having another kid so soon.

Meanwhile I've tried to type through a day of diaper-changing, approaching my children with blinders on my eyes, buffers in my ears. Karl's not feeling well either, and how pathetic it is to watch him. There is no brave and postured lying. All the discomfort is written on his face, exuded in his lackluster, low-energy mood.

Only Noah and I seem to be ready to smile and laugh on this dark night.

February 28, 1967

Yesterday was my birthday. Foumi cooked a lovely *coq au vin* and *crème caramel,* and we had good Italian wine. Though it was still frightening, becoming thirty-nine wasn't as bad as I had anticipated.

March 26, 1967

Today we've had a scare, a psychological scare, and we're still affected by it. We took Noah to the pediatrician for his third triple shot. We thought the visit would be routine. While there we told the doctor that we were slightly worried because Noah, now almost nine months, still does not sit up or turn over by himself. We expected the doctor to tell us that we had nothing to worry about, that we were being overanxious parents.

But instead he asked us about Noah's speech—which is negligible. And whether Noah could pass objects from hand to hand—which he can't. He then voiced concern about Noah's motor development, suggesting that if Noah did not start to develop significantly within the next three months, we ought to have a specialist look at him. Afterward, in his office he tried to reassure us, saying that it was "strictly a gut reaction" but he didn't think we had anything to really worry about because everything else about Noah was so healthy. But we came home and began looking at Noah through worried eyes, and it was easy to see a mongoloid idiot lurking in his beautiful Eurasian face. The good doctor having allowed how it might be a good idea to try to coax his motor development along, we exercised Noah almost mercilessly. But then he wouldn't eat at all. Foumi and I kept trying out new diagnoses and prognoses on each other. We both feel so guilty. We've never really given Noah the time and the attention we gave his brother. But we thought that is the way with second children: they simply demand and require less.

To add to our guilt, there is also the fact that we did not want Noah. The pregnancy came less than a year after Karl's birth. We would have had an abortion except we were broke, just newly returned to the country, coupled with the fact that a close friend had just told us of her harrowing and sleazy experience going through an abortion mill. So perhaps Noah sensed chemically in the womb that he wasn't welcome. Perhaps that's why he even frequently vomited his milk during his first few weeks of life—as if to reject the life that had initially wanted to reject him.

March 27, 1967

Noah seems to be more agile today. We tell each other hourly that we are worrying less and less. But not until he stands or turns over will we really relax and cry happily. In what we hope is not his—and our—adversity, our love pours out to him; he looks all the more beautiful in his potential helplessness. My instinct—historically so

19

unreliable—tells me he's all right. Noah is so lovely: he will look so much lovelier when he sits up. But if he is a case of arrested motor development, if gradually his form of retardation manifests itself increasingly, I will not love him a mite less, and he will be even more my son.

March 28, 1967

Karl grows, spouts words, makes jokes, is more and more trouble and more and more fun. Oh, that Noah achieves that state! I think he's got a problem with some of the muscles in his lower back. Perhaps he'll need a brace for a while, and maybe later a slight operation. But that's all I think it is. And he came out of the womb early. They always say babies who come out a week early are always at least a month behind. I hope so.

March 30, 1967

I could almost swear Noah seems to be moving about more.

April 7, 1967

Karl was funny this morning. For weeks and weeks he's been looking forward to going to "school." So I took him to "school"—the church day-care nursery—and he cried until I took him home. Foumi thinks it's because he knew he would be making a bowel movement. I think it's because he didn't like the idea of leaving Noah home alone to receive all the affection and attention of Mama and Papa. Which shows how Foumi and I basically differ in our interpretations of cosmic events.

I just received a late bulletin from the playroom to the effect that Noah is almost standing. The news thrilled me, but I replied in my best W. C. Fields tone: "When the kid walks, I'll come look."

April 8, 1967

Karl surprises me with his budding intelligence—his ability to tie together and relate different experiences. Getting into the car this morning he noticed that the light goes on when the door opens—"just like the refrigerator."

April 11, 1967

I notice that when Noah tries to move one hand, to grasp something with it, the other hand strains and his eyes keep blinking as if a message were being gobbled by nerve endings.

April 13, 1967

What kind of a writer am I? Here it is one o'clock, and I'm just getting to my typewriter. I'll tell you what kind of writer I am—I'm a father-writer. This morning we took Noah to the doctor for his smallpox shot. The doctor observed again in passing that it "was strictly a gut reaction," but he was sure Noah would eventually develop normally.

And now, after lunch, while Noah is napping, Karl is bouncing about my study, banging on the closet doors, his cookie box on the floor near my feet as a sort of home base which he keeps returning to and then wandering. away from, a wafer richer.

Even if Karl is cute and Noah is cuddly, on days like this they're both downright drags.

April 15, 1967

It is almost midnight, and I'm sucking in on a nipple, a milk-bottle nipple, trying to break it in for Noah. He doesn't like new hard nipples; he likes them soft and worn with use. So I suck on his nipple, enjoying the parental role reversal and turnabout in a primordial way.

April 16, 1967

We've decided to stop worrying about Noah. He isn't retarded, he's just pushing the clock hands about at his own slow speed. Yet . . .

April 17, 1967

It's *just spring*—like in E. E. Cummings' poem— trees budding, flowers blooming *far and wee*, and I feel eternally *balloon man* young. And yet at the same time my baby boys cry out death to me. "You will die," says Karl, as he crawls all over me. "You will perish," says Noah, as he clings to my shoulders. "We will grow big and you will become small—so small you will disappear," they say in chorus.

April 19, 1967

At about this time every evening as I attend to these pages I hear the insect-like buzzing of my fluorescent desk lamp and the trains passing down near the foot of the river and Noah shrieking gleefully upstairs. And then I half-shudder. There is something joyous about his cries, but there is also something frightening.

April 26, 1967

Oh, how my sons fill me with an asexual love for Foumi that I never imagined possible.

Here comes Karl, all two and a half years old of him, stumble-running through the corridor, opening the door, and arriving at my desk with an overbrimming smile on his face. Then he runs out again, and I hear Noah gurgle-laughing. I'm a lucky man. In a job, I would always be between phone rings, or hold buttons, having to carry on make-work conversations.

May 19, 1967

Last night we burned some of the twigs that lay about our yard, clearing the land like pioneers. But Karl was a pain, falling down, wandering off toward the poison ivy, insisting that we button up the bottom of his pants. My next child will be a robot.

June 7, 1967

Noah's running a fever, not quite himself. Whenever he's sick, I feel as if I'm on a losing streak or in a demoralizing slump.

This evening was a doubleheader of children trouble. I was playing with Karl on the driveway, letting him run toward me, when he stumbled, fell, bounced upon his upper lip, and came up a bloody mess of dirt and crying. I carried him into the house, where Noah was just vomiting. We cleaned the kids up and I called the doctor. He was out, but his answering service referred us to a "colleague," who suggested we come right over.

We did. She examined the boys, found Karl more frightened than wounded, and thought she detected signs of an ear infection in Noah. She also took a throat smear to check out the possibility of a strep throat.

Now I hope the boys sleep quietly, without disturbing me, because I have to stay up all night to meet a bloody deadline.

Noah doesn't have a strep throat, the doctor reported over the phone, though she thinks he might have roseola. I looked in Spock. Roseola is no great worry.

Just before dinner Foumi really flew at me. Inadvertently I had stepped on a patch of earth she was cultivating. I did so chasing after Karl, who was busy smearing himself with a jar of Vaseline. Foumi was so indignant that I had trampled upon the lives of her incipient flowers that she refused to prepare dinner. So I tried to make sukiyaki myself and screwed up terribly. That frustrated me, and I became impatient with Karl over a trifle and clouted him. It was justice of a sort, I guess. I had suffered because of him at the hands of Foumi. Now, because of Foumi he suffered at my hands. But later, undressing him for bed, I tried to make affectionate amends. And I realized suddenly that no matter how much I love Noah, Karl has a head start on my love that Noah can never catch up with.

July 1, 1967

This morning on awakening we gathered around Noah's crib, Foumi and I, and sang Happy Birthday. Karl refused to join in. But Noah joyously acknowledged it all with a few giddy bounces.

July 18, 1967

More and more Vietnam occupies my thoughts. But I'm also wondering if I'm allowing it to become the diversionary cosmic problem one plays with instead of the more pressing personal problem one must deal with.

July 24, 1967

Yesterday we went to a cookout at some friends who are summering near here. They're nice kids, and it's a sad thing that has happened to them: their first child is retarded.

August 3, 1967

We still have our Noah problem. He does not as yet turn over by himself. But by lying more and more on his stomach I think perhaps he is developing the strength and firmness in the proper muscles.

August 8, 1967

The day is dark, cloudy, heavy, pregnant with summer rain. I yearn for the morning sounds of the boys already. It is always such a joy to see Karl and Noah when they first awake, when they smile and start to chatter, happy to discover the miracle of a new day. Karl asks a simple question; Noah baby-cries out some simple request; and we all sit down to a messy breakfast together.

August 16, 1967

We took Noah to a pediatrician in the next town, who specializes in neurology. He said that since Noah is talking now there was little cause to worry; that Noah seemed "hypertonic," a floppy baby, a slow developer, but that time would be the maturing agent. We came away relieved. But I also have to admit that lately I haven't been worried that much.

August 22, 1967

We thought we might as well keep the appointment we had scheduled with a pediatrician neurologist in the city. We woke at seven into grayness, put out the garbage, dressed the kids, and organized for our drive there.

The specialist's examination of Noah seemed to fall in thoroughness somewhere between that of our regular pediatrician and that of the pediatrician in the next town. We expected more reassurance. Instead we received more cause for concern. He thinks that Noah's slow motor development—which is what has been primarily worrying us—may be symptomatic of intellectual retardation as well.

So we left with a new problem and a more vexing one. But not before the doctor ordered a series of x-rays of Noah's skull and brain. And that was, it turned out, an ordeal. When we arrived at the x-ray room the technician told me to come with her, leaving Foumi and Karl in the waiting room. Then she briskly began to weigh Noah down with sandbags on the x-ray table and asked me to place weighted bars about his face to keep his head in place. This technique didn't work, she botched up a series of x-rays, and cruelly began to push Noah about, when I suggested she get Foumi. The technician, young, dumb-faced, close-mouthed, vacuously chewing gum, finally said: "Okay." It was obvious the girl didn't know what to do, but I didn't quite know how to stop her. Foumi did. She had the presence of mind in the x-ray room to instruct the girl that only patience—not force—could do the job.

Finally, the x-rays taken, we went to the cafeteria and as always managed to enjoy Karl's pleasure at eating in a public place. He called out to me proudly: "Josh." And he ate as if he were performing an act of great skill for an audience. Which, indeed, he was.

Back home, Foumi and I, unable to sleep, talked into the night about Noah. And in the morning we were still caught up in that reality. We constantly looked into Noah's eyes for signs of light; we tried to observe his every movement for a hint of great development; we looked for obvious faults in that doctor, as if he were the messenger in a Greek play.

Foumi refuses to believe that it is possible for Noah to be retarded. But why should the doctor want to shock us? I think he's playing out the possibilities, and he wouldn't be unless there were enough indications in Noah's tardy motor development to warrant doing so.

It is hard to look at your own baby and say he may not be normal. But I think we have to. To us, of course, a child is healthy until proven unhealthy; to the specialist the child is retarded until proven normal.

Yet how I wonder what my approach should be. Consider Noah normal until the sword falls? Or consider him possibly retarded until the burden lightens?

Meanwhile, waiting for the x-ray results, we know they may show nothing, and still our worries cannot be allayed. The pediatrician-neurologist predicts Noah will eventually walk and he will talk increasingly. Yet talking, the doctor says, is not enough. For just as slow motor development is the classic sign of mental retardation, he says the intellectual-capabilities gap only widens as the child ages. If, for example, right now Noah functions like a normal baby half his age, projecting this ratio forward, he winds up with an IQ of 50—or less.

September 1, 1967

I spoke to our local pediatrician. He reminded us of his "strictly gut reaction," that there was not much cause to worry about Noah, that he was probably just a slow developer who would turn out all right. So we spent the evening playing with Noah most pleasurably.

I've noticed something about Noah. He requires my attention, my playing with him. He will refuse to grow without my love. I hope to make time to hold him on my lap, to fondle and hug him, to make him feel sure—and secure—in the knowledge that he is wanted wholeheartedly, enthusiastically. I must constantly be aware that he is the younger child whose sensitivities—and problems—are harder to discover than the firstborn's.

I've been reading child-care books. It seems I've been doing everything wrong: arguing with Karl, ignoring Noah. And have discovered I am not very "self-regulated."

Over the weekend I tried to regulate myself, to pay equal attention to both boys, and to treat them with equanimity. It didn't quite work out. Noah, who has come to life, asked for precisely what he wanted. But whatever he wanted, Karl wanted too, often not only competing in the demand but also escalating it. Soon I was arguing with Karl again, ignoring Noah once more, and definitively deciding that I was not very "self-regulated."

September 19, 1967

Noah, a little more than a year old, is of course still in diapers. But Karl, almost three, has been on his way out of them. This morning, though, he wet the floor and refused to try to use the bathroom himself. And now he is running around naked asking for diapers "just like Noah." I don't want to force anything, but I don't want him to regress either.

September 25, 1967

Thankfully, the weather has been lovely, clear but cool; the river is beginning to break through the trees and we can see slivers of it meeting the sky; and rising up like mud pies, farther on, the shore on the other side. The fall flowers, the marigolds and the chrysanthemums, are blooming cheerfully, and there is still the happy sound of birds. And Karl makes all the sounds of conversation, while Noah is still quietly beautiful and relatively immobile.

September 27, 1967

I played with Noah a good deal today, delighting at his standing with my help. But the world is still a bloody mess, the opposition to the war in Vietnam is sporadic and unofficial and just doesn't have a chance. I noticed today the RESIST ad running in the *New Republic* and the *New York Review of Books*, my name duly inscribed among the list of signatories. I don't see what good it will do my country—or rather what good it will make my country do—but it does soothe my soul.

October 8, 1967

Noah is more of a baby and Karl is more of a boy, and they have both been bawling all day demanding their rights, rights impossible to render them: the right to undivided attention.

October 13, 1967

Noah still strikes me as sluggish, apathetic, not very alert. But Foumi's convinced he's all right. I worry about him in a deep way. Karl is a problem, but a usual one. He's always challenging my authority, and I have to be careful not to challenge too traumatically his right to challenge it.

November 2, 1967

Foumi went to the doctor today—a rainy, black day —and I watched the kids and soon understood what was wrong with her—the kids. I began to feel my own stomach walls bloated and inflamed, an ulcer forming there, from the tension of having to deal with them all day long. And Foumi has to go through this day after day. Karl has the energy of a pile driver and the destructive capabilities of a bulldozer; and Noah, in his way, is always ready to crawl-slam into TV sets or knock over plants.

The doctor told Foumi to get help in the house and to get me out of the house. He said that was the only way to preserve our health and to save our marriage. And I think he's right. I'll get an office.

November 15, 1967

It's winter cold, below freezing, and the night promises to be even colder. I played with Noah and Karl for a while, and then I got bored. Foumi seems to have the patience to stay with them much longer than I can. After a little mutual affection, a few laughs, I want them off me, and I want to get on and do my things.

Now the sounds of Karl and Noah, fighting and crying, Foumi interceding. The sounds of my home, my life. My things.

November 17, 1967

I took Karl to the community nursery school for his audition. He seemed sufficiently smart and alert to qualify. The only trouble is, he isn't really completely toilet-trained yet.

November 18, 1967

We picked up training pants today for Karl—and Noah. Foumi thinks we can do both jobs at the same time.

November 26, 1967

Karl is three years old today, Noah one year, five months, and twenty-six days. And they're both celebrating the occasion by showing off their new toilet-training prowess. They have both been progressing magnificently. Karl has urination licked. And Noah will defecate—or urinate—right if we catch him. So with Karl set to go to nursery school in January, I guess the pyramid of life is beginning, the process of estrangement setting in. And it's about time.

Yet—oh, how they can still fill me with joy at certain moments. With Karl I can be affectionate and know I'm bespeaking my love demonstratively to him. But with Noah it's a different story. Sometimes just looking at him is a rare aesthetic experience, and I want to communicate my love for him but don't quite know how to. Simply hugging him, I know, is not enough, for somehow that just doesn't get through to his core.

December 4, 1967

Karl is now big enough for me to get angry at in a paternal way. Foumi can't quite understand how fathers take their sons seriously. But when he infuriates me, I am infuriated. I forget he's only a three-year-old. So I manfully had to control myself all morning. Because Karl was terrible today. When I was dressing him this morning he cried about the sweater he would have to wear, and he must have cried another half-dozen times by noon. Noah, meanwhile, was cute as hell, continually calling out: "Dosh." It's as if he knows that every time he says my name I thrill as though he were reciting all the Aeneid in dactylic hexameter. He helped save his brother a few angry blows this morning.

December 7, 1967

I rented an office, but I did not go there. Instead I took

Karl for a ride today, feeling that he is fighting an uphill battle in trying to attract interest away from Noah.

December 21, 1967

We visited Foumi's brother and his family, recently settled in Riverdale. Karl behaved quietly and respectfully, enjoying his older cousins, thirteen and fifteen. I recalled how much, as a boy, I enjoyed the company of my older male cousins. And looking at my nephews, I also sensed, in a vivid way, foreshadowings of my own sons, preview performances, that were both pleasing and displeasing, satisfying and confusing at the same time.

January 17, 1968

Sending Karl to nursery school has sort of dominated our lives. We have to wake up to the ring of an alarm clock, which makes sleeping a bit more difficult for us. I love going to bed late and hate deadline sleeping. Nursery school may be good for Karl, but I'm just not sure if it's worth it for us. While Karl becomes more alert, we may wind up insomniacs.

Noah, too, does not help gentle our nights. Last night, for example, he woke up crying, and we took him into bed with us, but he still kept making noises until well into the ding-a-ling morning.

January 20, 1968

The wages of preschool nurseries are sickness. Karl has the mumps. I guess Noah's next. And Foumi and I aren't feeling too well either.

February 13, 1968

We all seem well now, winter colds and mumps all
gone. But still the problems of parent-being and child-rear-
ing. Last night I was playing with Noah and having great
fun. And then Karl came barrel-tumbling along. And the
joy went out of our play. Noah rarely gets a chance to
play with me alone, so I became angry with Karl. And it
showed. The poor kid was miserable. To make matters
worse, I was so hostile that I even teased him. I must remember not to be cruel with one kid just because he inter-
feres with my love for the other.

February 15, 1968

Karl amazes and delights us daily with his vocabulary
and language construction. But today Foumi and I took
time out to worry about Noah. Foumi feels that perhaps he
isn't getting enough calcium into his system. We'll try to
give him some. His teeth do look bad, weak, as if there is
some sort of deficiency. And I do think he's a rather frail,
if tough-spirited, boy.

March 9, 1968

Noah bounces more and more. And soon, with the
change of season, I hope he will bounce to his feet.

March 11, 1968

Noah kept us all up half the night, giggling to himself
and bouncing in his crib. I became annoyed with him and
finally slapped him. He laughed back at me.

35

March 26, 1968

Noah is sick. There's a pinkish tinge to his urine, and he always seems to have a slight fever. I'm worried about him. I always seem to be worrying about him. Perhaps that's why when I feel he's well he delights me inordinately. Karl may be a master of words, but Noah is a tyrant of moods. He is deep too: inscrutable—there is no other word for him. He is quick to copy, quick to react, but impossible when it comes to figuring out just what he's thinking.

April 5, 1968

The killing of Martin Luther King last night has shocked me into complete inactivity. King's death, of course, makes one reconsider one's life and wonder what it is precisely that one is living for and exactly what it is that one might be willing to die for. But no matter what one decides, no matter how much one tends to moralize after the fact, a death like that of King, like that of John Kennedy, is senseless. And there is no way to purge such deaths of their senselessness.

April 10, 1968

On this lovely sunny-budding-spring day—I know it, I feel it—by summer or fall Noah will be walking.

April 24, 1968

Karl is alternately a delight and an impossibility. One moment he's surprisingly understanding, the next moment an unadulterated and selfish bastard. I guess that's being three.

May 28, 1968

Yesterday I took Foumi to the chiropractor's. The ambience of his office seems phony, the machines look derived out of science fiction, childish and roboty, and the diagrams looked liked Paris Metro maps. When he spoke he used words like "okey doke" and "righto." But Foumi says his snaps have made her neck feel better. Perhaps we should let him give Noah a few treatments.

June 5, 1968

The terrible immortality of a Kennedy. The weather is lovely summer, but not the heart of it, and Bobby Kennedy was shot. I keep looking at the front-page picture of him, sprawled on the hotel kitchen floor. Lying near death, it is as if he is near birth. And it strikes me, almost uncannily, he looks a bit like Noah.

What do we do to ourselves in this country, what madnesses do we give birth to, that we are forever stepping forward to kill each other?

June 10, 1968

Noah talks delightfully as he continues to crawl about on his honkers rather than his belly. My nephews, says Foumi, crawled in the same way.

Today I drove Karl and Noah to the lake. Karl stared at the sand at the water's edge and poked at it. Noah held on

37

to my legs and shyly looked out at the lake, giggling. I was so full of love for both of them it was almost obscene.

June 13, 1968

Noah is coming along in terms of coordination. He all but eats by himself now, especially if we fill his spoon, dental-assistant style.

July 1, 1968

Noah is two. He still doesn't walk, but I do think he's trying to teach himself how to stand up. We're still concerned. And I guess we'll remain concerned until he stands up and walks like a boy.

July 3, 1968

Last night, watching the "Les Crane Show," and listening to Linus Pauling discuss megavitamin dosages for the treatment of mental illness, Foumi and I began to wonder again if Noah might have some sort of vitamin deficiency that retards him—or if he's just plain retarded after all. Foumi senses once more something emotionally strange about him. There is his otherworldly beauty, there is his inscrutable opacity. Sometimes I can call his name ten times and he won't even turn around.

July 10, 1968

I behaved badly with Karl last night. Just after I had gone to sleep he awoke crying. And I treated him roughly instead of tenderly.

Meanwhile Noah is becoming bouncier and bouncier, like a squirrel, climbing stairs and atop of couches and trying to stand up on mattresses. He'll be able to walk soon, and then we realize the real problem will begin: how to contain him?

And in the street he calls out the names of all the children and greets them with a big "Hi," as if he were running for public office instead of walking along with the hand-holding support of his father. Yet sometimes I can still call his name a dozen times and he won't respond.

July 25, 1968

Today we worried: Noah didn't urinate all day. But finally after almost twenty hours he relieved himself.

July 29, 1968

Noah's been moody, crying for great periods. Foumi thinks he might be sick, have a kidney ailment. I think it's his teeth.

August 3, 1968

Noah still may be weak on his feet, but he's awfully strong when it comes to will. Suddenly frustrated at a meal when he's not receiving the attention he deems he deserves, he'll throw his plate on the floor. Then he'll fling himself on the floor too and go into a temper tantrum.

Karl also hasn't been Mr. Serenity of late. Twice yesterday he punched members of the family. Once Foumi—a hard shot to the stomach; once Noah—a sneak hammer blow on the back while the kid was crawling.

August 11, 1968

A hint of fall, a reverse Keatsian day. It is still warm, but the humidity is gone, the sinuses are cleared, and one is lulled by the weather rather than affronted by it. This morning I whisper-dressed Karl, and we had a quiet men's breakfast together. Then came Foumi, Noah, and our masculine camaraderie dissipated itself into the beginning of another family day.

August 29, 1968

Noah is sick, fevered, his eyes dull: a throat virus. To add to the gloom, there is the Democratic Convention. Now we are beating up kids at home as well as killing Asians abroad.

September 8, 1968

Let's face it: Noah has temper tantrums, he does not walk by himself, he is unable to talk too coherently. We live in a shadow of doubt and worry about him constantly.

September 11, 1968

Noah had a b.m. on his plastic toilet seat. And he was so proud of himself for doing so. I looked at his face, and it was as if some of the beauty seemed to have vanished from it. And I was glad.

September 12, 1968

The fate of a self-employed writer. The first day of school, I took Karl to his new nursery school. I was the only man among mothers. And I could see them all regarding me strangely, querulously, wondering if I were unemployed, divorced, separated, a poor relation. The reason I accompanied Karl was that Foumi was so tired. Noah had kept her up half the night crying. That kid can really throw a tantrum. But he's also pretty bright. At least, that's what I keep telling myself.

September 17, 1968

I did not take Karl to school this morning. He is so high-strung and uptight about school that it has backfired into a cold. Noah, meanwhile, is finally, matter-of-factly growing up. He sits at the table at breakfast, industriously happy, supremely involved, picking the corn flakes out of his bowl. Then he looks over to me and smiles and demands juice ("more juice") or bread ("I want bread"). And at night he tries to stumble-walk across our bed.

September 23, 1968

Noah walked all by himself today for the first time. Hallelujah!

October 3, 1968

This morning, at Karl's request, I took Noah along as I drove him to school. And at school I let Noah stand in the kindergarten classroom for a second, surrounded by Karl's curious classmates. He was both thrilled and embarrassed, his giggling head ducking down behind his shoulder.

Noah matures daily. Last night he promenaded about the playroom with a ball in his hand, averting nonexistent tacklers. I so delight in seeing him walk about by himself and in listening to him talk. He is on his way at last to becoming a nonbaby.

There was a sort of PTA night at Karl's school. We went and learned about him as if he were another person. His teacher spoke of the fact that the other children enjoyed his sense of humor and his love of laughter. His behavior at home would never have told us that.

It is cold, prewinter. It will be a night to spend at home with my boys. God, what a pleasure it is to play with them on my bed. Karl is growing into a creature who has a life in the world, an identity outside of his home. And Noah seems to be continuing that great transformation from baby to boy. Oh, how I hope his long babyhood is over. The simple mechanics involved in babying him are so hard for Foumi. Just to pick him up, for instance. She weighs only eighty-eight pounds, and he's already almost one-third of that.

Last night I heard Karl crying: "I can't see. I can't see." I got out of bed and went to see what it was. His light was out. But so too were the rest of the lights in the house. Then Noah began to cry too. I phoned the electric company and learned that it was a power failure, another blackout. I brought Noah and Karl to our beds. And so, in the Con Edison-spawned quilted community, Noah laughing and talking, Karl coughing and squirming, we all ineffectually tried to sleep. I'm glad today is Sunday.

November 22, 1968

There has been a series of phone calls between here and Foumi's brother in Riverdale and her family in Japan. Her father evidently has cancer, bone cancer. For the past few months we had heard reports, first of mucus in the chest, next a pain in the leg, and then that he had broken a shoulder bone while in bed in the hospital. Foumi's brother Yutaka had called a Japanese doctor here. He suggested it all sounded like Big C. Yutaka called Japan. It is.

Foumi received the phone call, the last phone call from her brother, laughing almost lightly. I was relieved, sure we had all misjudged the omens. Until she hung up and began to cry and told me the news.

This is her first intimation of her own mortality. I feel sorry for her. I also feel sorry for her father. But now his imminent death, just as the death of my mother while we were abroad, seems to stitch our lives, Foumi's and mine, ever so much closer together. At this point it's hard to tell my fabric from Foumi's. Death, as much as love, makes us literally one.

The critical illness of an in-law is a strange sensation. One knows the person because of a role, but there is no feeling quotient assigned to the role. I like my father-in-

43

law, in Japan we got along well, always sipping *sake* quietly together. He is a nice, polite, precise, proper, stubborn, arrogant little man. I shall never forget my first sight of him, Foumi pointing him out to me from the ship's deck, waving up to us tentatively, on that cold day we sailed into Kobe. I shall always remember his trying to make me more comfortable, to put me more at my ease no matter how great the effort was for him to do so, especially when it came to speaking English. And I realize his extreme gentleness when I compare him to almost anyone that I know in America.

Foumi and I spoke of what will happen to her younger brother, to her mother back in Japan. But mostly I hope that he is not in too much pain; for pain is the warning buzzer that clears the tracks for death.

November 23, 1968

The death of a parent is hard enough, but when the first parent who faces death is the father, it is much harder—I think for a woman as well as a man. Foumi didn't sleep much last night; I tried to comfort her as best I could, but this morning she was still crying.

November 25, 1968

Tomorrow Karl will be four. He is still lovely and playful, but now he's beginning to exhibit a personality. And it is not unlike the personality I had. He wants to be a joker, he likes to make others laugh. It must be something in the genes; my father was like that too.

And Noah is flourishing; every day he seems to take a giant step. I've given up trying to count his vocabulary. I think he knows words he doesn't even use.

November 30, 1968

Karl is four years old. At one moment he seems more like a boy, the next moment more like a baby. He alternates between being pliably affectionate and rigidly obstinate. I guess he's trying out roles. Noah is deep—or stupid. We still can't figure out which. But whatever he is, he does give us a completely baby kind of joy. Still I hope I soon will miss not having a baby in the house.

December 1, 1968

Putting Karl to bed, I argued too vehemently with him. Foumi raises her voice, and the children submit. I threaten too easily, cajole too much, play my aces too soon. They know I'm volatile and do not respect me for it. But why should I want and demand respect from them ever—let alone at the ages of four and two? I'm a bloody fool. I still don't know how to exercise authority; I only know how to bemoan against it.

December 10, 1968

It was a cold day at breakfast. I exploded against Foumi, against her lack of system in preparing breakfast. Eight years of marriage, and she still doesn't know how to set the table. I huffed and I puffed, and Noah responded by spill-

45

ing first his cereal and then his juice. And Karl point-blank refused to come down the stairs.

We started the new year off at the party of our Okinawan friend in a nearby town. There was the comfort and ease that comes from tradition. There was a surfeit of *sashimi* and *sushi* and all manner of good Japanese food. Karl was given little toys to play with, and Noah was a constant delight, parading about the room in his usual circular route, dipping for potato chips, parting people as they sat on the floor around the long banquet table. It was a good way to start the year.

Karl has become a bigger boy. He now puts his toys away, stacked somehow both neatly and creatively at the same time. But Noah remains a puzzle. He seldom sleeps; he never seems to listen to us. All of his sensitivities seem directed only toward himself. This morning Noah threw his juice on the floor. But he did not cry when we chastised him. Nor did he cry when I threatened not to take him with me for a car ride this morning. He hears only what he wants to hear, communicates only what he cares to.

Foumi's concerned about Noah again. But I just don't want to start the new year with the same old problem: worrying about the kid.

Noah has come to my desk and wants to type
He massages the keys so lovingly.
  and he knows how to work the space bar
  AND HE CAN WORK THE SHIFT
and he PResses the tab   noah jiro greenfeld
Now Karl has come. They're fighting over the typewriter.

My sons: Karl is truth. He looks like a boy, reacts without deviousness, his life never that far from the surface. Noah is beauty, sensitive rather than sensible, his life throbbing away in some subcellar. Karl laughs, audibly, openly. Noah smiles, silently, mysteriously.

Last evening the definitive phone call. Foumi's father is dead. And Foumi was on the verge of tears for most of the night. If I would hold her she would cry; if she held on to me, she did not cry. I let her cling to me, choosing her own form of comforting, until the kids were up and it was time to start a new day.

Foumi slowly, inevitably, I think, is absorbing the fact of her father's death. And I must not be so protective of Noah. After Karl pushed him down this morning, I pushed Karl over.

February 14, 1969

It's St. Valentine's day, and I'm going to massacre Karl. All day he's been bugging me about a racing car. Yes, I've told him a thousand times, I will get him a racing car. (And I will. I will.) But every moment there is a lull in his life he brings the matter up. And there seem to be lulls every seven seconds.

February 15, 1969

I bought Karl an ambulance. He had been asking for a racing car, getting on my nerves with his requests. I even yelled at him so sharply when I left the house this morning to go into town that he was reduced to crying, head flung down on the couch. I looked all over town for a racing car, but I couldn't find one. So finally I settled for an ambulance and brought it home. I expected tears of disappointment. Instead I was greeted by shrieks of joy. He was happy with his toy, and I was even more delighted by his new adaptability. No moral. Or is there?

February 27, 1969

My forty-first birthday: I am too cynical to dream anymore, but still too dreamy to be cynical. I play with the boys on my bed. Noah goes off to his room for a moment. Then he hears Karl and me having fun. He rushes back with a cry of the wounded, the jealously aggrieved, and proceeds to hug and strike out at me at the same time. I spend a great deal of time with the boys. Why not? They are the celebration of my life.

I was born, I have been told, on a snowy day. Perhaps

that is why when I think of my own childhood I first think of snowy days and frost on the windowpanes, and the announcement over the radio: No School Today. And then after a leisurely breakfast of my favorite foods (crackers and cream cheese and Droste's cocoa) I look out the Jack Frost windows and see that the sun has begun to come out after all and that it will be a bonus day, a gift from the city. I dress and go outside and play in the snow. I decide that I will dig to China. I have the impression that if I dig a hole deep enough I will get to China. I have tried before to dig to China, but the ground has always been too hard for my little shovel. I have been waiting for just such a snowy day, the snow piled high on the driveway, for I know snow is easy to dig into. And so I dig through the snow until I reach the hard gravel-topped driveway. I still do not get to China.

But there are other memories, memories of summer and my father. I am four years old, the same age as Karl is now, and we are at the beach in Revere, Massachusetts, hand holding hand, standing at the water's edge. I look past his thigh out into the ocean. And I hear his voice above me patiently answering my questions: "On the other side of that water is Europe." "Can I walk there?" I ask. "No, the water gets over your head." "Can I swim there then?" He laughs. "Not unless you become a very good swimmer." "I am a very good swimmer," I say, and charge forward and lie down and begin to splash in the ankle-deep water. And he laughs. I do not ask him: "What is Europe?" I know Europe is where he comes from. Which makes it ever so much nearer than China.

Afterward we are in the public bathhouse. It is a big and special treat to change bathing suits together, to shower together, to walk over the wood grating together, to be allowed to hold the key to the locker. Oh, what a thrill it is to be with my father alone. Away from my mother and sister. Just my father and me. Only the boys in the family. Our exclusive society.

It is a Sunday afternoon. Only my father and I get into the car. We drive to Boston in the maroon Chevy flivver and go to a baseball game. We sit on the splintery wood benches of the old Braves park bleachers. I love to go to baseball games with my father. Only the boys in the family. Our own special community.

I have a baseball glove. I walk over to the chicken slaughterhouse my father operates, throwing a taped baseball in the air, taking the shortcut that skirts the edge of the beginning of the city dump, past a pile of telephone poles that lie log-cabin style on the ground. My father volunteers to have a catch with me. And when he throws the ball I try not to notice that he throws like a girl.

My boys, now sleeping in their rooms upstairs—what memories of childhood, what memories of me, are they storing away in their winter sit-by-the-fire treasure troughs?

March 23, 1969

Sunday evening. The family is gathered in the playroom —Foumi reading the paper, Karl playing with his blocks, Noah wandering his route. And Lassie is barking up a storm on television.

April 24, 1969

Now that it is spring we notice that Noah seemed to withdraw and regress more and more through winter. He refuses to listen, or to understand what we say to him, and has all but stopped talking. It's time to see a doctor again.

May 2, 1969

Foumi is worried. Not only does Noah continue to show a lack of progress, but he has stopped progressing at all, in fact, has regressed. He talks less now than he did two years ago. I'm afraid to go to a doctor because I know that we'll then find out whatever the specialist knows. Expertise discovers itself in its subjects.

June 2, 1969

Noah has the chickenpox, and Foumi's mother has come from Japan. Maybe we were wrong to invite her to America. At first the children were enthralled with her; now they're bored. And since she's unable to speak a word of English, she's so scared that she won't stray an inch from the house. Not yet, anyway.

June 6, 1969

Our fears about Noah continue to undergo dramatic ups and downs. Because of his increased opacity, the fact that he doesn't respond when we call his name and fails to relate completely to his immediate environment—a pattern of retardation or autism—we took him to a nearby hospital. There, in a team approach, a child psychologist, a psychiatrist, and a speech therapist will all test him and then compare notes. The doctor in charge of the overall program preexamined Noah. She used phrases such as "autistic tendencies" to describe him, thus intensifying our worst fears. Especially Foumi's. In her heart she knows something is wrong with Noah. What disturbs her most are his sudden outbursts of laughter. I guess we both fear that what we dread is so, that Noah is not a normal child, that he is a freak, and his condition is getting worse.

June 7, 1969

All day yesterday there were tears beneath my eyes, waiting to stream through the facade of workaday reality. On the train into the city I wanted to cry. But of course I couldn't. And I didn't know what good crying would do. Finally everything surfaced when I got home. Foumi and I got into a senseless argument as to whether hereditary factors were the cause of Noah's possible—indeed, very likely—retardation or autism.

June 9, 1969

Today I am less emotional but more aware of the fact that the problem does exist. Noah is a burden, withdrawing in steps; the moments of connection, of entry into the outer world, becoming less and less. Perhaps it is me, my presence at his side, that he needs the most. Perhaps I should not begrudge him a moment of my time from now on.

We both rack our brains trying to figure out just when he began to stop talking. Foumi recalls now how Noah fell a few times on our hard playroom floor last autumn. Afterward he kept saying: "Oh, my head!" And he never said much after that. She thinks those falls might have something to do with his regression. Or perhaps, she thinks, it was the cold weather, the literally cold world, which froze his fragile sensitivities. Meanwhile he cried and had tantrums, making no other effort to communicate when he was unhappy. Fortunately, though, he is usually joyously, vacuously, absently happy. But I do so wish we could reach him.

June 16, 1969

When I stay home all day and observe Noah constantly it becomes apparent to me that he is a disturbed child. I cannot get angry with him. I cannot get angry with myself. I cannot get angry with Foumi. But she can get angry with both me and America. Wanting children in general was always a vanity of mine; she did not want to have any children at all. She particularly did not want to have a child when she was pregnant with Noah. But being broke and in America, an abortion could not be too seriously considered at the time. So she damns the country where the church forces the irrational to occur—childbirth when one does not want it—and me for my sentimentality, my desire to have children. Also we wonder about the obstetrician now: did she induce Noah's birth too early? Did she slip Foumi an anesthetic? Did she deprive Noah of proper womb nourishment by insisting that the eighty-eight-pound Foumi diet?

Karl matures daily; now he dresses himself. And the gulf between him and Noah, between normal progression and abnormal regression or retardation, broadens. It will be hard to bring Karl up with Noah about.

Shit! I wish we had not induced him. But all the pieces fit together: born early, a vomiter rejecting external reality, a furtive laugher, delayed motor development. And my vanity. I thought that by marrying outside of my race that bad genes—the diabetes on my father's side, the mental illness of cousins on my mother's side—could be eliminated. Instead, I have further scattered bad genes.

Foumi seems to make the adjustment better than I do. I play intellectual games. I try to feel that Noah must have some wondrous perceptions, that in some way he is ahead of us all. But I also do not fool myself. I know deep down that he has a life doomed to grotesque development.

June 20, 1969

We took Noah to the hospital to receive his EEG. But then he refused to go to sleep under sedation, and the crotchety old nun became more and more flustered. Finally we called off the test. And after a lunch in the hospital cafeteria, during which Noah tossed plates and cups around, we retreated home. Here we don't have to worry about flying objects beheading other people. We've all learned to be ready to duck at all times.

June 26, 1969

Yesterday I took Noah to the chiropractor. I don't know what black magic the man can perform, but he is gentle, easygoing, and does seem sympathetically aware of Noah. I also spoke with the doctor at the hospital. She said we'd bypass the EEG testing for now.

I am in North Africa, in Marrakesh on a magazine assignment, and I've just senselessly called home to wish Noah a happy birthday. Today he is three. I spoke to Foumi and missed her intensely. I spoke to Karl and missed him gnawingly. I could not speak to Noah and missed him most of all.

We saw another pediatrician-neurologist in New York. We had made an appointment with this specialist for September. But when a last-minute cancellation opened up, we accepted it. And after briefly examining Noah, the eminent doctor offered his verdict: Noah was a classical retardate. However, he couldn't reconcile within his diagnosis the fact that Noah was talking by the age of one and had stopped talking at about two and a half. ("In that case," the doctor allowed, "his retardation is not so classical.") And suggested that we ought to put Noah in the hospital for a few days of intensive diagnostic testing.

Foumi and I have been mulling the matter over. Should we subject Noah to tests now? What could such tests show? For unless such tests can detect a progressively deteriorating condition that they know how to check, we might as well wait before hospitalizing Noah.

Last night I called an old friend who's head of a university psychology department and told him about Noah. He was sober and professional, offering little advice but listening well. But just before I hung up he surprised me by asking if it was all right for him to tell his wife about Noah. Of course it was, I said.

The fate of Noah hangs over us like a joke whose grim punchline one vaguely remembers having heard before. But even as we know Noah's retarded, we still can't believe there is no hope, and so we look for little outs, random possibilities that might upset the diagnostic apple cart. And there is the fact that once he spoke, although his speaking, to be sure, was rarely a two-way street: he communicated sentences, but never allowed verbal notions to intrude upon him. Or is this all part of our foolish-parent imaginations? Did Noah merely ape sounds before he could walk, and never really talk at all? No. He did utter sentences that did have relevancy to the moment in terms of his wants and needs.

Just because we know his behavior is deviant by a wide mark from the norm, that he is the world's oldest baby, a bundle of infant babyhood whose actions are like those of one less than half his age, I see no point to putting him in the hospital now. Why pay to discover what we already know?

Somehow the rhythm of our lives, the good fortune of our marriage, seems to have dissipated. It is hard for Foumi to believe in me and for me to believe in Foumi anymore. Successful monogamy, of course, must be based on a faith in the union if nothing else. And how can we have faith in a marriage that has biologically backfired? Foumi is traditionally so self-protective that the moment she does not protect herself she has no luck. And though she claims the Freudian dialectics do not apply to her, she teems with guilt toward herself and accusations toward me. And I guess I act the same way toward her. In any event, our house of good cards has fallen apart. At first I thought the news of Noah would stabilize and fix and reaffirm our marriage. Now I'm not so sure.

It is ironic, though, that Foumi and I, who both believe so in beauty and have enjoyed such a rare aesthetic experience in Noah, are thus reminded of the absurd mindlessness of it all.

July 15, 1969

I've spent the day looking at the otherworldly Noah in the playroom and watching the man in the moon launch on television and trying to evaluate both. I am convinced that although Noah is obviously backward and retarded, there is an emotional base at the root of his problems: he has withdrawn into our fears.

There was also something eerie about the moon shot. The simulated animation seemed no less real than the real thing.

July 16, 1969

The neurologist sent his report to our pediatrician:

ATTENDING ADMISSION NOTE
NOAH GREENFELD

This is the first examination of this three-year-old youngster who is admitted with the chief complaint of delayed acquisition of developmental milestones complicated by regression involving expressive language function.

Noah is the result of a nine-month uncomplicated pregnancy that was terminated by induction of labor and a normal delivery. The birth weight was 7 lbs., 11 oz. The immediate neonatal period was characterized by a weak suck at the breast. In addition, there was recurrent vomiting for the first month of life.

The acquisition of developmental milestones revealed a significant delay in motor milestones in that the child sat alone at 8 months, crawled at 18 months, stood alone unassisted at 2 years, 3 months, and walked unassisted also at 2 years, 3 months. Noah first began to speak with words at 8 months of age; in phrases at 18 months, and also spoke in complete sentences at 18 months of age. Shortly after he began to walk at 2 years, 3 months, he stopped speaking. In addition, for the past 8 months he has ceased to be responsive to his immediate environment.

Coordination is stated to be average for walking, running, and throwing. The child is not yet toilet-trained.

Past medical history and review of systems revealed that Noah had mumps and chickenpox before the age of three, and the parents have noted that the urine is pink since the first year of age.

Behaviorally the youngster is stated to have a low frustration threshold, poor attention span, temper outbursts, is impulsive and underactive, and has multiple fears.

The family history is essentially negative.

Physical examination revealed a youngster who showed no true purposeful activity, and his motor function was often without direction. The child would jump up and down or on other occasions stare inappropriately at his right hand. On occasion the child babbled, but this babble was without inflection. At no time was there any evidence of true expressive language patterns.

His head circumference measured 49.8cm. and there was no evidence of an intracranial bruit. The occiput was flattened. The gait was on a wide base with a tendency to toe outward. This gait was associated with a prominent hypotonia and associated hyperextensibility of joints. This decrease in muscle tone was present in both the upper and lower extremities. The hypotonia was associated with hyperreflexia; this was more prominent in the lower extremities. The Babinski responses were normal. There were no pathological reflexes. Sensory examination was normal to touch and pain. Cranial nerve examination and the funduscopic evaluation was benign.

IMPRESSION: Atonic diplegia—the evidence to support this clinical impression is the prominent hypotonia associated with marked hyperreflexia and psychomotor retardation. The history of regression as evidenced by loss of previously acquired speech patterns is most unusual in this condition, and the possibility of a degenerative disease of the central nervous system must be ruled out.

July 18, 1969

How to treat Noah? How should I behave toward him? I do not think that I should say "No" or "Bad boy" to him. Rather I should encourage him for his good behavior. Because he may be not only retarded but also complicatedly emotionally withdrawn. Perhaps that sensitive little doll of a human being is so afraid of me that he has decided to cut himself off from a world in which I rant and rave so. I'll play with him tonight as gently as I can.

July 19, 1969

No matter how severe Noah's retardation, I refuse to view his condition as a life-searing tragedy. We will do what we have to do. We will take care of him as best we can until we can no longer take care of him. We will have him in our home and find ways to live in joy with him. And when I cannot enjoy him as much as I would like to, I will love him even more.

July 22, 1969

I watched the astronauts take their first wraithlike steps on the moon. But there were two bigger events during the day for our family. First, Noah urinated after twenty-four hours of watery silence. Second, in the morning I talked to our pediatrician. The gist of our discussion was most depressing. He seems to feel that if Noah is not simply retarded, then he is suffering from a degenerative brain disease, something esoteric and rare of the neuromuscular variety. He therefore thinks we should hospitalize Noah immediately.

I called the neurologist. But he says there would be no great dramatic difference if we were to put off his observation of Noah for a while. So I think we'll hold back the black dawn for a month.

But it also occurs to me now that if Noah is really suffering from some dread disease, I might want it to run its course—which could be death. But simply retardation, I no longer consider a tragic death blow to our lives. If he can talk, if he is educable and trainable, there yet might be a beautiful life in store for him with us. Or as beautiful as one can make the life of another whom one loves.

July 23, 1969

We were in the city, the family en masse, and walked through the streets of Greenwich Village. And I felt much as I had felt in walking through St. Germain in Paris three weeks ago: a kind of vibrancy of place that was especially refreshing after suburbia. The people were still obviously phony, but the place oozed potential. Walking along these streets were those who had proclaimed their search for life rather then their surrender to it. But the Village, as St. Germain, remains the staging area for those who can take off only according to standard operating procedures, set motifs. Like me. Unlike Foumi. For Foumi is someone who has—and has had—the courage to take off on her own. She did come to another country, to a different culture, all by herself.

July 24, 1969

Decisions are made by events, not people. I have been wondering what to do about Noah all week, whether to place him in the hospital right away or not. But when I called the neurologist's office to find out what tests he had in mind, his secretary informed me that it was impossible to book Noah into the hospital until September anyway. So my mulling has all been moot.

And now we have a schedule of sorts. In August Noah will receive his psychological checkup at the hospital near here, and in September he'll have his neurological testing in the city, where they will try to find out if he has a brain tumor, a clot, or some sort of degenerative neuromuscular disease.

Thus, at this point in his wee life I hope Noah is simply retarded—a hell of a thing to have to root for. But I also fear it is something more than that. How else can we explain the fact that he once spoke? If it's hard to accept Noah as he is, then it is even harder to look forward to the explanations.

July 27, 1969

If our star-blessed lives have fallen over onto the other side of the moon, we now have to pick ourselves up and move forward again, but this time without the comforting cop-out sense of Victorian progression. My beautiful son will lead me toward the awful truth after all.

August 1, 1969

Again we took Noah to the hospital near here that has a special children's unit. Noah did not speak to the speech therapist, and his behavior was generally below that of a one-year-old. But he gave her a ball when she asked for it. Which is more than he does for me.

The psychologist and the psychiatrist at the hospital thought it would be a good idea if they could observe Noah over a longer period of time in a play rather than an artificial testing situation. And since they have a summer-camp program there, Noah will go every day for the next three weeks. And perhaps afterward he will be admitted to the hospital as a day patient, attending their special school.

Meanwhile, last night, as I tried to fall asleep I heard Foumi crying. Why? She was crying for Karl, for the difficulties he would have with other children because he had an abnormal brother. I tried to comfort her, but I know she's right. Karl will have to be a remarkable kid to bear up under that load, and the most endearing thing about Karl is that he is so unremarkable. So typical, so average.

Indeed, now that a piece has fallen out of our smoothly scenarioed life, I have a much greater respect for the norm, the median standard, than I had hitherto dreamed. It is so much better than that which cannot help but be deviant.

But while Foumi seems convinced at this point that there is something irremediably wrong with Noah, I vacillate between the reality of my observations (he does not communicate, he does not relate) and the indomitability of my hope (he will mature, he will outgrow what is wrong).

August 8, 1969

I feel as if my sons are grown and have left the house: it is awesomely quiet. Noah has gone off to the hospital nursery day camp, and Karl is at his school's day camp.

We are pleased with the psychologist at the hospital, but we are not quite sure what they might discover about

63

Noah there. They seem to be trying the emotionally disturbed route. Foumi is sure it is brain damage, with perhaps a layer of emotional disturbance overriding it. Obviously it is rather pronounced—whatever it is—or it wouldn't evince itself so early.

But this morning when I took Noah to meet the chauffeured station wagon that would take him to the hospital, I met the father of two older children, both cerebral-palsy victims in braces, who were also being picked up. He looked at the smiling, scrambling Noah and said jealously to me: "He doesn't seem very badly off."

Yet who knows what the future will show? Who knows how Noah yet might not develop? If he is all lovable one-year-old baby at three, the fact remains that one can never quite reach him, and most of his babbling has almost no relevancy. One cannot get him to give a simple reply, to come when he is called, or to return the slightest modicum of affection. He accepts hugging and kissing but offers up no token of his own love. There is an opaque barrier, a filter or a jell, that he places between himself and the world.

The world. . . . I have to climb back into it, to my workaday life there—even though nothing in it seems as important, or as absorbing, as Noah.

August 9, 1969

I played with an alert Karl, an indecipherable Noah. Whether his retardation is physiologically or psychologically derived, it seems he does not recognize places or people that strongly. If we have to put him away, perhaps he will not miss us, wherever we put him.

August 14, 1969

I drove Noah to the hospital today and talked to the psychologist there. She told me she'd be recommending Noah for their preschool program. Transportation would be a problem. But I told her we'll figure out how to handle that problem when we get to it.

The hospital itself, not surprisingly, reminds me of the hospital across the river I entered twenty-one years ago (this week?) after coming down with polio. There is no air of death about the place. Only the pathos of long-standing incurable illnesses. The Georgian design, the red brick, the wheelchair ramps, all enhance the *déjà vu* feeling. But now it is my son, not me, who is the victim.

August 17, 1969

When I look at Noah's fellow day campers at the hospital I simply do not want to associate Noah with them: I mean, their braces and their rolling heads and their anguished sounds. But he—emotionally disturbed or organically retarded—is one of them.

August 18, 1969

Last night we had dinner with two couples, both of whom have brain-damaged daughters in institutions now. They spoke of their experiences, the differing diagnoses, the physical and emotional difficulties imposed on the rest of the family. With slight deviations here and there, our experience with Noah seems to be following some sort of terrible master script.

One of the couples highly recommended a particular

Philadelphia neurologist and briefed us on the specific approach of "Patterning" of the Institutes for the Achievement of Human Potential there. It seems like a lot of work, but they said it was the only thing that seemed to work with their daughter before they had to commit her.

Foumi also spoke the other day over the phone to a woman in the next town who has an autistic son, eight years old, who is now in a state hospital. Foumi described Noah, and the woman said her son had been like that in most respects at the same age. Only he never talked. She advised us to simply enjoy Noah as much as we can while we can. "That's all," she said, "you can really do."

August 19, 1969

I spent the day in the library reading about all kinds of brain-damaged children. So this evening I've definitively diagnosed Noah as brain-damaged. Therefore the important thing is therapy. And the fact that the AMA-type doctor frowns upon "Patterning" makes me tend to regard it all the more favorably. I feel that it must be a lot like the Sister Kenny treatment was in polio: it may not get to the scientific heart of the problem, but it can make things a lot easier in terms of rehabilitation. Perhaps I should make an appointment for us in Philadelphia; it is something to consider—seriously.

August 21, 1969

I picked Noah up at the hospital today. He had just awakened and was in the hands of a teen-age volunteer. Noah looked toward me with sleepy eyes, and then his whole face lit up in a joyous smile. All of the volunteer counselors seem to love him. But Foumi has noticed that he has stopped walking for the most part since we've been sending him there. Most of his peers are cripples.

Noah, though, still does not seem interested in other children and talks progressively less. We are in more of a quandary. Should we make an appointment in Philadelphia? Or should we wait to find out what they say at the hospital near here first?

Decisions. Revisions. At the hospital I spoke with the mother of a child who seems the most like Noah will become. She told me that her son at six is still not toilet-trained, is under medication, and that she still has no clear idea of what causes his malfunctions. I guess we'll have to live with whatever ails Noah for a long time.

August 24, 1969

Yesterday felt like the first day of summer again. I took the kids to the lake in the afternoon, and I was pleased to see how much Karl had developed since last year. He could play by himself in the sand and was not afraid to go into the water. Noah was pretty much his withdrawn self, kicking sand about absently and crying when I carried him into the water. And then, standing at the water's edge, he urinated, the droplet stream sliding down his already wet leg.

My pendulum of instinct about Noah has once again swung back to a diagnosis of emotional disturbance. But as Foumi says, my thoughts usually depend on the last book I've read.

Perhaps. But most of my reading lately has been about

Patterning. The theory behind it is that crawling on the stomach and creeping on hands and knees—activities that Noah never really did—activate through physical stimulation the brain cells responsible for neurological development. In the normal development process a child first crawls homolaterally, or one side at a time, left arm and left leg move forward, then right arm and right leg. Next the child crawls in a cross pattern, right arm and left leg, left arm and right leg moving forward together. And when he walks and runs, of course, it is in a cross pattern too, the opposite legs and arms always moving at the same time. According to the patterning people, the brain is like a computer which must be programmed in steps. And cross patterning is the vital input that triggers open the cells in the developing sections of the brain responsible for a multitude of basic activities ranging from the creation and appreciation of meaningful sounds to depth perception. "Patterning" therapy or treatment usually works this way: the child is made to crawl or creep something like eight times a day for five-minute periods (separated by at least half-hour intervals), during which teams of three to five people manipulate the child's arms and legs and head in the desired movements or patterns, thus indelibly etching the pattern of crawling into the brain and activating the cells onto higher developmental stages. "Patterning" is not so much a belief that man cannot walk until he crawls as it is a conviction that man cannot even drawl until he crawls. But "Patterning," alas, in theory and practice, with all its promise does not pretend to apply to the psychotic brain. And Noah at this time, I strongly suspect, is nothing if not psychotic.

September 1, 1969

Lately everybody has been telling us their problems. Friends confide that their marriage is on the rocks, even casual dinner companions fill us in with all the details of their difficulties. It is as if now that it is obvious we have a great problem on our hands, we somehow also must be equipped with great reservoirs of compassion and understanding. Unfortunately, not so.

September 3, 1969

Last night Foumi and I were talking about guilt, trying to define it simply. It is a lack of definition of oneself, we finally decided, a childish dependence upon the values of others. It is no accident that religion and parents, the great institutionalized sentimentalities and authorities, give guilt.

Today I've decided, wavering again in my amateur diagnostic attempts, that Noah's difficulty is brain damage. Anyway, in a few days we'll have a conference at the hospital about him. I don't quite know what we'll learn from it, but I have a hunch . . . nothing. Probably further neurological tests will be called for. Somehow the prism of the future remains bent and crooked.

September 5, 1969

Karl and I alternately fight and hug each other. Today he was funny. I read to him a Chinese fortune-cookie prediction: "Success will visit you soon." Immediately he began crying, obviously very frightened. Finally he explained the reason for his tears. He thought Success was a monster of some sort.

And I think of Noah continually, each day coming up with a new diagnosis. Today he was a bit more social and babbled a great deal, and I've decided that he has some sort of emotional disturbance based upon a minimal kind of brain damage. Tomorrow the professional Noah handicappers will deliver their verdict.

Meanwhile, I guess I'm a Jewish mother—imprisoned in every thin Jewish father is a fat Jewish mother completely dominating his personality—in the way I fret over him.

September 6, 1969

We had our conference with the team at the hospital. Nothing really surprising emerged. They think Noah is primarily emotionally disturbed. They doubt that he is brain-damaged, because there are no striking corroborative symptoms, such as drooling, accompanying his speech regression. And speech, or rather its absence, is the basic form of regression, the sure sign of a withdrawal syndrome. Where do we go from here? We'll have him checked out again neurologically, this time with a neurologist who is supposed to be psychologically oriented. And they suggested that we send Noah to a school for retarded children—which is about two miles from where we live —rather than to their hospital school, as we had anticipated. But it is apparent that there is no clear pattern of action for us to follow. For example, I asked the psychologist and the psychiatrist separately whether we should treat Noah's "misconducts" leniently or strictly. I got opposite answers. I asked the question because Karl has been complaining about the double standard around our house: why does he have to put away things when Noah doesn't?

And explain as we might, it's difficult for Karl's four-year-old mind to accept. Poor kid. He will have enough troubles being a Eurasian and a Jew-Jap without the additional burden of having a "crazy" or "dopey" brother. Sometimes I try to prepare to inure him against the epithets that will certainly come. But at the moment his instinct for sibling rivalry is greater than his capacity to reason or understand. And that's to be expected.

He and Noah get along in their own way, rolling like kittens sometimes on the floor or bed. But then Karl might sneak punch him, and Noah rarely defends himself, just turns away as if he is interested in something else.

Yet Karl identifies with Noah to a scary degree. Sometimes, when Noah suddenly decides he does not want to continue a walk and just sits himself down on the street and refuses to budge, I say: "Okay, Noah. I'll leave you here." And start to walk away. But then Karl gets hysterical: "Bring him. Bring Noah." And stands there next to him wailing.

September 13, 1969

I'm a lousy father. I anger too easily. I get hot with Karl and take on a four-year-old kid. I shout at Noah and further upset an already disturbed one. Perhaps I'm responsible for Noah's problems. Perhaps he would be better off if I were to take off. It may be something worth trying. If I am a failure as a father, then I should face it.

September 14, 1969

Last night some friends came over with their three young children. And Noah, I think, seemed to begin to take some tentative steps out of his shell. But watching our friends' two-year-old son, so animatedly alive, I realized again how far back Noah is, how much he has to go forward. I must stop talking sharply to him, I must be gentle with him, I must realize that he is as delicate as a reed, as fragile as rice paper.

September 20, 1969

Foumi says Noah's been behaving better, improving almost daily. He's been holding in his urine until we put him on the john, so perhaps we might be able to toilet-train him eventually. Oh, that everything wrong about him could be due merely to a slow developmental pace, things that time will right.

September 27, 1969

For several days we had some high hopes about Noah, but we were simply self-hypnotically trying to lull ourselves into a dream state. He's resisting the toilet again, throwing his spoons away, holding fast in almost every way to whatever it is that shuts him off from our world. Yet I love him to a point where my heart almost breaks. Later, he will be a grotesque, but now he is beauty in its richest, most fleeting sense. And to think that I have contributed to such beauty draws me to it even more. In a

Death in Venice way I do not think I could desert him even if it meant my own doom.

October 2, 1969

The team at the hospital kept insisting that we make an appointment with the County Mental Health people. We went to them yesterday. They thought we wanted therapy for ourselves. No, we told the nice social worker there, we want advice about Noah. Oh, she said, there must be some misunderstanding, and sent us home.

October 4, 1969

The psychologist member of the hospital team called. She said we need therapy, that's what the appointment with the County Mental Health people was all about.

Foumi told her: nonsense. I said I'm not resistant to the idea of therapy, I would enter it myself—without Foumi—if it could possibly help Noah. The psychologist said: no, to be effective you should both enter it. Afterward Foumi and I quarreled. But she was adamant; she refuses to participate in anything which is such an obvious waste of time.

October 6, 1969

I took a brood of children, including Noah, to the zoo, and bought them all Cracker Jacks and balloons. It was fun to watch all the kids having fun. Except Noah—he couldn't care less. In his long camel-hair coat he was like a little king wandering through his own captionless comic strip, one that lacked a last panel.

October 7, 1969

We visited the nearby school for retardates, a red-brick building set in the side of a hill, like a bunker. There is little space. In a railroad-flat setup they have three classes: younger children, older children, and adult retardates. The classes for the children look like happy bedlams, mongoloids running around, kids screaming, their muscles twitching. We came in time to watch one of the adult retardates celebrate his birthday; the singing of "Happy Birthday," the blowing out of the candles, the serving of the ice cream and cake. Of course, they were all like children, those close-eyed, sweetly vacuous heads. I almost cried. I refused to imagine that Noah, my son, belonged in such a place, with such a group.

The school was formed by a group of local working people, built by them brick by brick, because there were simply no facilities around for retarded children. It's the only game in town, and we are grateful it exists and that they've accepted Noah.

October 14, 1969

I had lunch with a friend today who was telling me of his problems with his nine-year-old daughter, how she doesn't like school, how she's so rebellious. "I'm worried about her," he told me; "she needs therapy. I think the child is seriously disturbed."

"Buddy," I said, "don't use words loosely; you don't know when you're well off."

October 15, 1969

The Vietnam Moratorium was a great outpouring of the young, but a lot of exercise for someone who is aging like myself. And I came home and learned that Noah has a running stomach and Karl a bad cough. And soon I wasn't feeling too well myself either. But what the hell? The leaves are golden and red and fall in clusters that shred like tobacco, the air is clear, the weather pre-stinging cool, and I'm home with the family again. And that, I guess, is all that really matters to me.

October 22, 1969

Once more to a new neurologist. Once more to the testing line for Noah. Last night I dreamt Noah was a twenty-year-old who could talk but at times could also transport himself into being a two-year-old who could not talk—a ˙capsule expression, I guess, of both my wishes and my fears.

October 28, 1969

We took Noah for some more tests, including another EEG. We saw other children like him—or like he will become. I really have little hope that he will ever be much more than he is. Perhaps when he gets older he will talk a little, seem more social, but basically he will never be unlocked from his autistic self.

November 11, 1969

For days we've been trying to catch Noah's urine and bottle it. Today he surrendered. And I rush-chauffeured it over to the hospital lab so it might be tested. Negative. But I also received some bad news. The EEG he took again on his visit to the neurologist last month hadn't taken. So I'm supposed to bring him back for another.

Last night I went to a meeting at his school. It may have to close, it is out of funds, and the staff has been placed temporarily on two-thirds salary. I volunteered to help fund-raise.

Meanwhile, I'm worried about Noah's fate. I went and spoke to the County Mental Health people, to the social worker there. There is no way they can be of any help to us. She didn't even know what facilities the state has to offer for a child like Noah, let alone what special schools existed in the county. But again she was ready to refer me to therapy. Bullshit!

November 26, 1969

It is Karl's birthday. How swiftly our lives seemed to have passed—or evolved—since that day he was born in Kobe five years ago. I remember sensing a new life for us all. But how could I anticipate the coming of a Noah? If it is my lousy genes, how could I have known my genes were that lousy?

November 27, 1969

Karl is watching the Thanksgiving Day parades on television, and he's disappointed in our turkey now roasting in the oven. "It doesn't look like a turkey—where are the feathers?" And Noah's staging a parade of his own, just promenading endlessly in a circular path about the perimeter of the playroom.

I've been thinking about the irony of Noah. I was glad when Karl was born that my son was of the future, the mixed race bag of the future. But perhaps Noah in his way is the real grim example of the future, the schizophrenic future.

Meanwhile, though, we still have to face the prejudicial present. Foumi finds it almost impossible to get help. Both black and white domestics and mothers' helpers do not like to work for an oriental woman. And Noah's condition just compounds the problem. No one likes to take care of a problem kid.

December 15, 1969
Noah talks: today he kept repeating the words "My son, my son" over and over again. Funny boy. Crazy kid. In a way perhaps he's what every parent secretly yearns for: a child who'll never grow up.

December 24, 1969
Foumi manages to maintain her calm, her equilibrium. But because of Noah, my lines of self-projection have become murky and tangled. And on this Christmas Eve I find myself depressed, thinking most unhappily about Noah.

For example, I would like to leave this country for a while. It is time we traveled again. But how does one travel about the world with a mentally ill child in tow? And Noah is indeed schizophrenic; to spend time with him is to spend time with insanity. And it's catching. Sometimes I even think Noah is my own insanity walking, my cursed other-self inflicted upon my own second son. A dreary thought on a bright night, the Christmas tree lit in the corner making even an eternal Jew yearn to be a *goy* forever.

January 1, 1970

I was up half the night, first ministering to Karl and then trying to cater to Noah. The kid is crazy. We have to do something about him. But what? He bounces in his bed laughingly whenever he is wet. He laughs back when I bawl him out. He has drifted farther away from us than ever before. And because of him nothing seems to make sense anymore. I know these are the best days with him. I know I love him. I know he is beautiful. And I know my love for him—and his beauty—does not mean a goddamned thing.

I also notice that I have become more distrustful of Foumi, have lost some of my faith in her, so necessary for our marriage, for any marriage, because she has borne me Noah. Even though genetically, I suspect, it is I who am the cause. But worse than cheating or mutual suspicion when it comes to unfixing the mystique that glues a marriage, I guess, is to have a disturbed kid. At first I thought it would draw us closer together, necessarily cement our relationship. Now Foumi and I have to be wary that it doesn't draw us apart. We have to be intelligent enough to realize there is a strain on any marriage whenever a baby is sick. And we always have a sick baby.

January 6, 1970

What is my dream? My dream is that somehow Noah slowly improves, and everything else, all other dreams, are contingent upon that. But how will he improve? In the past year he has become noticeably worse, scarcely bothering to communicate at all anymore. Perhaps Noah has found a way to rule the family through dependence? In that case I doubt if he will surrender it.

January 7, 1970

I spoke to the director of Noah's school. She talked about County Mental Health and how Foumi and I could use some "guidance" when it comes to working with Noah and Karl. I listened to her. But then when I got home and repeated it all to Foumi, I realized how much nonsense it all was—at least as far as we're concerned. Noah, she pointed out, is schizophrenic, and the Freudians simply have no treatment for him. So what's the point of getting involved with them?

But we do have an appointment I set up a long time ago with an old Viennese lady doctor whom an analyst friend of mine recommended as "the gal to see about childhood disturbances." "If I had a problem like you have with your son," he said, "that's the gal I would see." Perhaps she might provide us with an evaluation that will prove helpful.

What I want at this point is a long-term prognosis. I would like to be able to plan ahead for even the worst eventuality.

Meanwhile I bring Noah to his school every day. In spite of the primitive conditions and the primordial behavior—the head banging, the twitching, the screaming—he seems to enjoy it.

This is the coldest day of the year, and we awoke to find Noah with a 103-degree temperature and reeking of diarrhea. Oh, how I hate to see him physically ill, so profoundly lost in complete misery and unable to be comforted through communication.

It's pretty hard to communicate to pediatricians, too. Noah refuses to take any oral medication, no matter how syrupy-tasting. But to get these guys to give Noah a shot takes a major effort. It's hard to make them realize that we won't hold them responsible if Noah winds up a junkie.

This has been the week of weeks, trying not our souls but our all too wispy flesh. First Noah, and then the rest of us, all came down with the flu. Foumi and I could barely move, and still there were the sick kids to take care of.

We were prepared to see the Viennese child psychoanalyst. But a few days ago her secretary called to say that there had been a fire in her study, so she could not take on any new patients at this time. Where do we go now? Back to the neurologists? Or should I go into psychotherapy —something I've successfully avoided all my life? We still assign blame to each other, Foumi and I, at angry moments over Noah. So many should-haves: we never should have had children, we should have protected ourselves, we should have aborted him. Guilt, thy name is "should have."

February 2, 1970

A word, a note, a lament: I have pneumonia. So the doctor told me.

February 8, 1970

I think I'm getting better; the chest pains are subsiding, but I'm going to nurse myself gradually, not push or pull or strain. No sense rushing into pleurisy. I just pray now that Noah gives me the grace of a night or two of uninterrupted sleep.

February 17, 1970

I'm recovered, back to my old dreamstand. I dream of Noah's progressing to a stage where he might be educable. But there really haven't been any signs of significant progress for a long time. And I feel so damned helpless.

Noah still governs my moods. If he seems happy, then I am. If he seems upset, then I am. But perhaps the truth of it is the other way around.

February 19, 1970

Foumi keeps complaining about how it's impossible to keep Noah from being destructive about the house. Anything on a table, in a cabinet, on a floor is fodder for him to break. Poor Foumi, she can't afford to take her eyes off him for a second. Poor Noah.

February 20, 1970

Perhaps we should still check Noah out with an analyst. My old analyst friend has recommended someone else.

February 22, 1970

Today I think that Noah is more retarded than emotionally disturbed, that he stopped talking because with his meager resources he simply couldn't cope with both talking and walking. And I optimistically recall that just as the first neurologist predicted someday he would walk (as he has), the second neurologist indicated he was sure Noah someday would talk.

March 2, 1970

I have written the Bettelheim people, the Sonia Shankman Orthogenic School in Chicago, asking about the possibilities of placing Noah there. A reply came from the associate director telling me that they did not consider accepting children until after the age of 5½ or 6. They suggested that meanwhile I might get in touch with a school and child-development center administered by the Jewish Board of Guardians.

I called the Jewish Board of Guardians. They said they do not take children who are not verbal.

Beautiful. Like *Catch-22*. On the one hand, I'm always told that it's important a child like Noah get treatment early, while he still can be reached and before he's withdrawn completely. On the other hand, the treatment institutions say Noah is either too young or too far gone for treatment.

When I went to pick up Noah, the director of his school stopped me again and said she thought both Foumi and I need psychotherapy, arguing in passing that the psychologist's report from the hospital suggested that our marriage was "tenuous."

Driving home, I laughed to myself, recalling that when the psychologist at the hospital had asked me to describe our marriage I had said: "Like all marriages, ours, at best, is tenuous." Ever since college, when I heard a football coach use the word to describe a prospect's chances of making the team, "tenuous" has been like a private and secret joke word of mine.

But Foumi was furious when I told all this to her, reacting with oriental talons open. She was angry in principle. How dare one judge a marriage on the basis of a five-minute interview, brazenly offer so insulting an opinion with so little evaluation. I'm not sure if Foumi wasn't overreacting at the idea of therapy or treatment, but I also think she is justly annoyed at their attempts to turn the whole problem around. And I have to trust her instincts in these matters more than mine. Not being a product of the culture, she can spot the snares and delusions, all the bullshit in it, with a much keener eye—or nose—than I.

Once more we visited the "psychologically oriented neurologist" who told us last time that she felt Noah had an emotional disturbance "engrafted" upon an organic retardation. Now she seems convinced that if Noah has an organic retardation it is minimal. This made me feel good.

At least we have some idea of where not to begin looking for treatment for Noah. This also made me feel bad: it means we never should have gotten involved with neurologists. And I'm wondering if we ought not to get involved with psychiatrists either. Suppose psychiatrists tell us his emotional disturbance is "minimal." Does that mean Noah is automatically not suffering seriously from anything?

This morning, though, the director of Noah's school called and asked if she might make an appointment for us with the school's consulting psychiatrist. I told her I'd had enough of doctors, that I don't feel like looking for anything in the way of professional treatment or evaluation for a while, that I'd simply rather accept Noah as "strange" for the time being and let it go at that.

March 12, 1970

Foumi's been reading Adele Davis, the health-food dietician, who mentions vitamin C as a great ameliorative for schizophrenia. And she wondered if we ought to feed Noah vitamin C as if it were candy. She called our pediatrician and asked him about it: "All Noah will get out of it," he said, "is an expensive urination."

I sometimes suspect in a metaphysical way that if we let Noah go completely his own way, be permissive in every respect, that might be the best thing.

March 14, 1970

I've invited Foumi's mother here again. We need help taking care of Noah, and he certainly can use all the attention he can get. Why does he refuse to come out of his shell? Why is he afraid to face reality? Why is he so threatened? Is it because Karl and Foumi and I are such strong-willed people, so hard to budge, so difficult to crack, so impossible to break through to?

March 15, 1970

I called David, my old friend who's head of the psychology department at the university, and had a talk with him about analysts and psychiatrists. I asked him what he would do at this time if he had a child just like Noah. He said he wouldn't do anything at this time because there was nothing psychiatrists could do.

March 18, 1970

We tried vitamin-C-ing Noah on an amateur basis, giving him five grams within a twenty-four-hour period. He had a great bowel movement but otherwise no real effect. I guess we can't scare away his schizophrenia that easily.

March 23, 1970

Reexamining these notes yesterday I realized that the only event which occurred during that fall and winter when Noah stopped talking and started withdrawing that could possibly be termed traumatic was Foumi's father's death: is Noah's condition a product—or result—of those unresolved emotional worries?

March 25, 1970

Foumi laughs at the Freudian twinges at the roots of my impulses. But I made an appointment to see my analyst friend's analyst friend who specializes in children, even though I know there is little that can come out of a visit. I mean, they don't seem to know what to do with Noah after they've played their little note-taking games, anyway. They really have no treatment. And I'm sure the visit will be a waste of time. Still, one feels that one should do something. Anything.

And I will ask the doctor to give it to me straight, to level with me. If prospects of any sort of real cure are grim, we should be ready to institutionalize Noah immediately, because the longer we wait, the harder it will be to part with him.

Eventually Noah probably belongs in a home for the mentally ill. But what if treatment facilities are better in places for the mentally retarded? My head swirls. I am confused again.

March 27, 1970

Yesterday Karl said to me, "Daddy, I know the biggest number—it's affinity." I laughed loudly, overly enjoying it, perhaps because I realized Noah, bouncing on the couch next to me, might never bring me such goodies.

April 3, 1970

Noah yodels away, and Karl tries to imitate him. They both disturb me. Last night Noah didn't go to bed until one o'clock, but he never slept. Instead, he whimpered and whined in his high eerie pitch all night through. I hope Karl, who is at the imitative age, does not begin to copy Noah in that respect.

I canceled the appointment in town with the analyst-type psychiatrist. What's the use? Gradually a kind of helplessness has drifted into me. I think I have to accept Noah's condition as incurable and start from there.

Our resolve weakened and we went to see a psychiatrist who had observed Noah in school. He said he thought Noah was a combination of mental retardation and mental illness but would classify him as hopeful if we got the right guidance. Every time we brought up a specific problem he said that was something we could talk over—at a future date. Then we realized the "guidance" he was talking about was for us. I could see how he was trying to operate "dynamically" in a textbook sort of a way. But it also struck me as something like trying to affect the quality of a chicken salad by the study of chicken feathers. Not for me or Foumi. And I couldn't see how it could help Noah. He's no *Fifty-Minute Hour* problem.

College students killed, campuses are closed down, Nixon goes marching into Cambodia, and I have to worry about a single crazy kid. Between Kent State and Jackson and Vietnam and Noah, I don't know which is the most absurd—the neurotic public problems or my personal psychotic one.

Driving Noah to school this morning, I saw a motley band of student stragglers holding their homemade signs

("Next Week: Thailand") strung out along the highway. It was all very moving. But where will we move as a nation? How can I move as an individual?

May 13, 1970

Noah woke me twice last night. Once because he was wet and once because he's crazy. Foumi has a theory: the diabetic genes in my father's family have emerged as schizophrenia in Noah. She may be right.

May 15, 1970

Foumi thinks of finding the right diet for Noah. I still can't help but range along psychogenic lines, wondering first about the right emotional environment, a proper educational setup.

May 20, 1970

Noah has been crying each day when I bring him to his school, so today I brought him to the nearby Montessori School. The directoress was like so many other people, in regard to Noah. At first she seemed greatly attracted by the challenge, but then gradually she was bored by his lack of response. So after looking him over, she turned him down, saying: "I can't make contact with him." I sighed. If contact could be made with Noah, who needed her?

May 28, 1970

Foumi has read in the Federation of Homemakers *Newsletter*—published by a consumer organization she belongs to—of a psychiatrist in New York who's had success in prescribing megavitamin therapy for emotionally disturbed children. I called and made an appointment with him.

More and more I like the idea of a psychiatrist who is a man of science with an understanding and respect for the workings of biochemistry. Wasn't it Freud himself who said the cures for mental illness will most likely be uncovered in the field of biochemistry.

June 8, 1970

Foumi's gone shopping, and I'm baby-sitting. To take care of Noah for twenty minutes is to know how radically ill he is.

June 12, 1970

At dinner at a friend's last night a child-psychology professor we know socially asked if Noah cries real tears. I'd never thought about it. I checked at home. He cries tears, crocodile tears, which is an encouraging sign. It means he isn't holding that much in.

June 17, 1970

Today we had a conference with Noah's teacher at the school. She thinks Noah has had a good year, better than we think he's had. She told us that he's emerged a little, that he seems to relate a little more to the other children at circle time, that he's beginning to be pleased with himself when he performs a simple activity such as working with form boxes. We feel good about what she says, but we also wonder if she has to feel a sense of improvement in order to justify all her hard work.

So much for some of my past journal entries. Perhaps they're too much about my reactions and impressions and not enough about Noah's experiences and sufferings. But his is a world I am shut out from, mine is a world he has been unable to enter. He still spends most of his days in happy withdrawal, often smiling as if at some inner joke, as he makes his rounds of our house, always almost symbolically closing each door behind him. But then there are also days and nights when he has sudden fits of sadness that are uncontrollable and unbearable, as he writhes upon the floor or on his bed in utter and abject unhappiness. And he is forever completely unpredictable, weaving from side to side, foot to foot, squinting his eyes in either self-stimulation or hallucination. One moment he may take my hand and lead me to the refrigerator and point out precisely a food at the rear of the bottom shelf, a pleasing taste remembered from weeks ago. A moment later, however, he may be unable to recall having communicated that simple desire. I never know what synapses and short circuits are occurring in his mind, perceptionally or conceptually. I only know, as I have said, we are a world apart.

I also must note how very few people can actually understand our situation as a family, how they assume we are aloof when we tend not to accept or extend the usual social invitations. Nor have I mentioned the extra expenses a child like Noah entails—those are entries I keep in another book. But as he gets older, the figure we may have to pay each year for his special schooling approximates that of a college-education semester. Indeed, most states treat children like Noah as third-class citizens; instead of providing more money for their possible education and training, they actually provide less.

Yet such considerations have been comparatively minor ones. What has been shocking to me is the fact that until I had a child like Noah, I automatically believed in the institutions of organized medicine, private philanthropy, and public programs. Where there's an ill, I naïvely thought, there must be a way. Simply not so, I discovered. The school Noah has been attending, for example, does not have the operating capital to provide the mentally ill or mentally retarded child with the same full-time, one-on-one treatment therapy he so desperately needs in order to have even a slim chance of a future. As it turns out, the school is fundless, near bankruptcy.

Even more heartbreaking has been the three-year period it has taken us to pierce the organized-medicine, institutionalized-mental-health gauze curtain. Most doctors, if they were unable to prescribe any form of curative aid, did their best to deter us from seeking it. Freudian-oriented psychiatrists and psychologists, if ill-equipped to deal with the problems of those not verbal, tried to inflict great feelings of guilt upon us as all-too-vulnerable parents. Neurologists and pediatricians, if not having the foggiest notions about the effects of diet and nutrition, vitamins and enzymes and their biochemical workings would always suggest such forms of therapy are practiced only by quacks. And county mental-health boards, we discovered, who have charge of the moneys that might be spent helping children like Noah, usually tossed their skimpy fundings away through existing channels that do not offer proper treatment for children like Noah.

This summer, though, we were able to make a series of breakthroughs regarding Noah. First we placed him in the hands of a psychiatrist who believes in megavitamin therapy. The psychiatrist diagnosed Noah as a childhood schizophrenic, and under his supervision Noah is currently receiving large dosages of vitamins in an attempt to correct his chemical imbalances. From talking to other parents we've learned that this sort of treatment can yield encouraging results.

Second, we had heard of the operant-conditioning program developed at UCLA by Dr. Ivar Lovaas, a behavioristic form of therapy in which the child is actively prodded through rewards and punishments out of passive withdrawal and into language and communication. We were never sure it could apply to Noah because we were never sure about Noah's diagnosis, but on a visit to California we stopped off at UCLA. There, watching a therapist treating youngsters, we learned that the same techniques can work with childhood schizophrenics. More important, my wife spoke to the parent of a child with symptoms like Noah's who through his operant conditioning had developed to the point where he was functioning in the real world.

So finally we knew of two concrete treatment programs for Noah's problem—megavitamins and operant conditioning—that could enhance each other.

But I still don't know exactly what's wrong with Noah. I only know something is profoundly wrong with him. I still don't know what to do—I only know I must do whatever I possibly can. Although Noah is too young for an institution now, I know I must still accept the very real possibility of his eventual institutionalization. I also know I must try not to feel more sorry for myself than for Noah, but some days I forget.

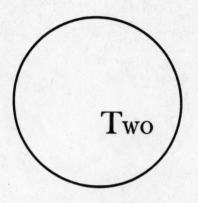

Two

August, 1971

. . . I still don't know exactly what's wrong with Noah. I only know something is profoundly wrong with him. I still don't know what to do—I only know I must do whatever I possibly can. Although Noah is too young for an institution now, I know I must still accept the very real possibility of his eventual institutionalization. I also know I must try not to feel more sorry for myself than for Noah, but some days I forget. . . .

It is a year, a long year, since I wrote these words about my autistic son, Noah. At that time he was four years old. He was neither toilet-trained nor could he feed himself; he seldom spoke expressively; his attention span was almost nil; he rarely played with toys at all; he never came when he was called by name; he was almost always lost in a world whose activities consisted solely of thread-pulling, lint-picking, blanket-sucking, spontaneous giggling, inexplicable crying, eye-squinting, finger-talking, wall-hugging, circle-walking, bed-bouncing, head-nodding, and body-rocking.

Now Noah is five. During the past year he has received megavitamin treatment—heavy dosages of certain vitamins daily—and been exposed intensively to operant conditioning, a behavioristic carrot-and-stick system of rewards and punishments. And things have changed: he has become easier to manage. He is out of diapers, and if he does not always tell us when he has to go to the bathroom, he will try to go when we tell him to. He plays with toys when prodded, winding up his music box or bouncing his Slinky, or pushing a car along the track on his Busy Box. He eats by himself and assists in his dressing, pulling on his socks and tugging up the zipper of his sleeper and poking his head through his T-shirts. He knows how to turn on the TV set and how to turn off the hot water in the bathtub.

Such feats may not seem the stuff of great otherworldly miracles, but judged in the context of the Noah we have known, we count each a blessing, marvelous as any grace. At the same time, though, we are too often reminded that Noah is still very much enclosed in a world of his own whose latch he makes not even the slightest attempt to jiggle—let alone lift. Again perhaps the best way for me to describe the experience of the past year, to communicate the changes in him—and us—the encouraging and hopeful baby steps forward he has made in certain directions and the sometimes agonizing and distressing lack of progress in other ways, is to go back and thumb through the pages of my journal.

Although the subject is little aware of it, a card from the chiropractor arrived informing us that today is Noah's fourth birthday. Noah had about a half-dozen chiropratic adjustments last fall—but with little effect. And when we saw that the chiropractor, for all of his good intentions, was gradually losing confidence in his treatments, was literally all but going through the motions, we stopped making appointments.

I set much greater store on Noah's daily regime of megavitamins. Diagnosed as a childhood schizophrenic—whatever that may mean—he now receives under the psychiatrist's supervision hefty doses of vitamins B-3, C, and E among other things, along with an enzyme-producing catalyst called Deanor. These vitamins come in pills which Foumi or I pulverize with a mortar and pestle and then spike into his orange juice.

We're also proceeding along the lines of the best workaday-live-through-the-week advice we've yet received in regard to Noah. It came from one of Dr. Lovaas' students at UCLA, Bob, an operant-conditioning therapist whom we met on our visit to UCLA. He told us to make Noah pay attention, establish eye contact, by saying, "Look at me." And to reward such "appropriate" behavior with a cookie or a potato chip. So whenever Noah starts jumping on the couch as he prepares to take off into his own world, or starts to prance-dance about a room, I shout: "Look at me." If he persists in his self-stimulation, in his inappropriate behavior, I admonish him with a sharp "No," a "Stop it," and even an occasional smack as Bob suggested.

But it takes an awful lot of persistent energy to keep after Noah. So we're beginning to think of moving to a place such as Los Angeles, which has a setup with the proper operant-conditioning facilities—and faculties. At the same time, we rebel at the idea of moving just because of Noah. We don't want to start dedicating our lives to him completely. We have three other lives in our family.

July 4, 1970

Noah awoke in an awful fit. For the first time he was self-destructive, reaching for his own eyes and trying to gouge them out, squeezing his testicles and painfully pulling at them, and lashing out at anyone who came near him. It was a frightening sight. We immediately called the megavitamin psychiatrist. He said not to be alarmed, that it all might be a good sign, that Noah's metabolism was probably changing, but that we still ought to take him off the vitamins for a few days. Which we're doing. But I wish he had warned us before of the possible initially explosive side effects.

July 6, 1970

When I brought Noah to the summer camp of his school this morning, I met the parent of another autistic child, a year older than Noah. I mentioned that we were considering moving. She has five other children, each with their own friends, their own schools, their own societies, she said, and so couldn't even begin to entertain the notion of moving. We're lucky; at least we have such options open to us.

July 8, 1970

Karl came home crying from his day camp. One of the other children had called him a "Chinese girl." And I don't know which offended him more, the noun or the adjective—or if any of it at all was meant to be pejorative.

July 15, 1970

We've reintroduced the vitamins one by one, gradually, increasing the dosage. And it seems it was the Deanor which caused the bad reaction, the crying fits and eye-rubbing and pinching. So we're decreasing the amount of Deanor.

July 19, 1970

This morning Foumi slept late, and I took Karl and Noah to the diner for breakfast. I think they liked it, sitting in a corner booth eating sloshy pancakes, but not as much as I did when I was a boy.

July 23, 1970

We went and looked over a new school that is opening for "exceptional children." The school is big in space and reeks with the smell of promise—but not of reality. At least for us: it is over on the other side of the county, thirty minutes away, and the logistics of transportation are considerable. Also the tuition. It's simply more than we can afford.

Meanwhile the days are hot, humid, muggy, and Noah is irritable, unable to understand the discomforts brought about by heat. But come to think of it, I'm irritable, and I *can* understand the discomforts.

August 1, 1970

We went to a meeting of the local National Autistic Society chapter. It was held in a meeting room above a bank, and like most of the meetings of Noah's school, the discussions for the most part had to do with fund-raising on a kind of church-social level. I don't see how they'll ever be able to finance a setup that can offer us more in terms of treatment for Noah than we can get at UCLA. So I think I'll begin to work out the mechanics of getting us to California for three or four months this winter.

August 3, 1970

I sat down with pencil and paper this morning and figured out our financial position. We can afford to give the UCLA approach a shot. And if we can't manage Noah any better afterward, if nothing seems to work there, then we'll have to think hard about institutionalizing him. Otherwise our lives will be one long servitude. And that's something we cannot afford.

August 4, 1970

Noah was impossible today, crying every other moment, scratching viciously, driving Foumi frantic. I discovered the summer volunteer helpers at Noah's school weren't giving him his vitamin medication. Which is more important than his going to school.

August 8, 1970

Foumi's been worried about Karl's coordination—or lack of it. So I especially scrutinized a five-year-old who came over to play with him yesterday. The kid was every bit as badly coordinated as Karl. I guess it's his age.

August 11, 1970

Noah does not let us sleep these nights. Whether it is the summer heat or the vitamin medication, I don't know. But we have to do something about him soon. Foumi is getting to the end of her tether.

August 12, 1970

Last night I took Noah for a long walk, and he slept well. Maybe he simply needs more exercise.

August 21, 1970

A lovely clear blue-skied day, and I decided to take the family to the zoo. I noticed something about Noah. He didn't seem to notice us at all. If we let him out of sight for a moment, he would attach himself to any adult thigh and wander away with it until I retrieved him. It was as if he did need *somebody*, but *anybody* would do. Not a very heart-warming feeling for a parent.

Foumi, out of guilt to both the young and the old, went into the city with her mother and Karl. I was left with Noah. Unremittingly. He had a b.m. and urinated twice, and except for a two-hour period in which I forced him to stay in his crib, he had me running, changing diapers, trying to curb his jumping, attempting to interest him in some kind of positive activity. I realized just how hard a day Foumi has every day.

A note came from UCLA. They won't exactly commit themselves to accepting Noah for therapy. They said if we'd come, they would see about it. But they all but intimated that they would accept Noah, though they would not accept the responsibility of telling us to come to California for just that purpose. I'm an old gambler; I'll take an "if-come" bet. We'll go to California.

I took Karl and Noah to a Labor Day picnic at a neighbor's. Karl was shy and retiring and would not mix with other children, hanging on me, and I could not help him mix because I was stuck to Noah. But Noah did talk a little, asking for juice ("I want juice"). He seems to be discovering again that it is possible for him to talk.

We went to see the vitamin doctor again. Not much was accomplished by the visit. But we do have a clearer view of Noah as a schizophrenic; and now we have to begin to have a clearer view of schizophrenia. The chances are indeed slim that Noah will ever be cured, as things stand now. But there always remains the chance that some day a biochemical cure will be found. In the doctor's waiting room we spoke to a schizophrenic of about twenty. She was blond and good-looking, and we noted how consciously she tried to talk. She said she lacked the ability to pay attention, to focus completely on any activity for very long, that it took her, for example, an hour to read a page in *Time* magazine. When she had schizophrenia attacks, she said, people were to her as things, assuming vague but threatening shapes. Since she has been receiving high dosages of vitamin C and Niacinimide, she told us, her attacks have become more infrequent. "Before, I used to have to have shock every couple of months, but now I can get by on just the vitamins."

The doctor also told us he would be getting a new vitamin he would like us to try on Noah—something that has been used with great success in the Soviet Union to help activate speech, B-15, which is supposed to help more oxygen get through to the brain cells.

September 10, 1970

The first day of regular school for both boys. Karl made excuses, said he was sick, didn't feel well, and cried. But once I got him into the car he was resigned to his fate. And when I parked behind the school he followed me timidly into his room, and there he joined the other kids, lining up docilely before the teacher's desk.

Next I took Noah to his school. And I was pleased to find that it had been painted cheerfully and to discover that the most disruptive noisemaker in his class was gone. I came back and told Foumi that it might not be a bad year for us after all.

September 15, 1970

Another note came from UCLA. Scarcely committing. I'm not sure anymore that I even want to go. I feel more faith in the vitamins than anything else, and I feel little faith in them.

September 18, 1970

This morning at breakfast I found my eggs too cold. Foumi couldn't understand how I could complain, considering Noah.

Considering Noah, I must bemoan for all the waste in her life. Her talents, her intelligence, her zest for travel. I must appreciate it and do something about it, instead of getting lost in my own bogs.

September 20, 1970

Foumi has read of a school in Connecticut. It would be easier to go there than to California.

September 25, 1970

What a night! Noah was up all of it. Two urinations, two b.m.'s, four diaper changes in all. And the period in between, he bounced and jumped and chirped.

Obviously Noah isn't making much headway; he has become more and more lax in his toilet training. And when I project, all I see is a sleepy life of never-ending diaper-changing for us all.

September 28, 1970

Perhaps we ought to get rid of Noah. No, that would not solve anything. There are always demanding mad-nesses in one's life. No, that's a madness too: to make of Noah a metaphor. But as Noah gets old . . .

October 1, 1970

We celebrated our tenth anniversary. We went into the city and had a good dinner at a Japanese restaurant and en-joyed Danielle Darrieux in *Coco*. More important, Foumi looked beautiful to me all day long.

October 3, 1970

Sometimes I feel Noah is part of a Faustian deal I've made but can scarcely recall. And most times he is more than I can bear—and bare. Right now he's having a run of diarrhea, is off vitamins, and Foumi is near the end of the line with him. Next week we'll investigate the school in Connecticut.

October 10, 1970

Foumi stayed in bed this Sunday morning; I dressed Noah and took him for a ride and then a walk. He was docile and amiable. Karl was the problem. He insisted on wearing his high-top sneakers, which weren't dry yet. He is stubborn, but what else would one expect from the son of Foumi and me?

October 12, 1970

Foumi is beginning to think that Karl too may be suffering from some kind of learning disability. That's all we need. But he is having a difficult time in the first grade. I think, though, it's just because he's one of the youngest in his class—not even six yet.

October 13, 1970

The truth about Noah is always depressing. Today was one of those days I could not avoid it, had to face it. We took him to a special school about ten miles from here which had been highly recommended to us. Again there were the forms to fill out, the questions to answer, and the patient examiners—in this case the director and a speech therapist. But again it was easy to see that they considered Noah a most difficult case, that there was little hope that they could hold out for him, and that though they were most sympathetic as people, they wanted no part of him professionally. In fact, they didn't even leave it on a don't-call-us-we'll-call-you basis. Instead, they said call us if you want. I asked, "When?" "In a week or two," was the vague response.

We'll go to Connecticut next week to look over the school there. And that will finish off our eastern investigation for the season. After Thanksgiving we'll be off to California.

Yesterday Noah. Today Karl. We went to his school and spoke with his teacher. She doesn't seem too concerned about his learning abilities—or rather, inabilities. She's sure he'll be all right. But we heave no heavy sighs of relief; we can't help but be hypochondriacs now when it comes to child development.

Noah was up again last night, whining in his high pitch that is so unbearable to me, each of his whelps going through me like a knife. Finally, I went downstairs to sleep.

October 15, 1970

I'm trying to keep all the options open. I'll call the people in our town who have a little girl in an institution they are satisfied with and find out how to apply for admission there for Noah. We may just have to institutionalize him when we come back from California. I simply can't see Foumi going through another year like this one. But damn Noah. The more time I spend with him, the more he evokes all the selfless love I am capable of, and sometimes he does relate to us individually.

At that school the other day the director asked: "What does Noah do all day?" It was hard to describe that Noah does nothing but sit or jump around. "And what happens if you don't feed him?" the speech therapist asked. "I don't know," said Foumi, "but some things I have to do just to make it easier for myself."

Yesterday Foumi, Karl, and Grandma went into the city to nibble at food and culture. I stayed behind with Noah, thinking it would be the least strain to take care of him. And it was, I guess. But he's hard to take over any extended spell. Time after time, for example, I'd bring him to the bathroom and he'd refuse to sit down on the toilet— and then he'd go in his pants. Perhaps that is normal for any rebellious four-year-old, but with all of his abnormalities, such normalities are an indulgence we can't afford.

Indeed, this past weekend has convinced me that we will have to get Noah out of the house soon for our own survival. Long ago he became too heavy for Foumi to lift physically. Now he's become too heavy for me to bear spiritually.

We went to see the school in Connecticut. It's the best setup we've seen yet. An old Tudor stucco building at the edge of a park, with its own enclosed playground. The director is the mother of an autistic child herself. She understands the problems of a Noah implicitly. She has one teacher per pupil, has the school doors open fifty-two weeks a year, from 9:30 A.M. to 4:30 P.M., six days a week. Most special schools don't realize that since they are for special children they require special hours. Because these kids just can't go home and run around and play after school and cavort all summer long. They don't know how to.

We would have to move to Connecticut if we were to send Noah there. But right now Noah is too young for both the school and the director's educational theories. She believes—and she is a former teacher herself—that it is much easier to work with older kids. The youngest student in her school is seven.

But the physical layout of the place—the gym, the private instructional booths, the abundance of teachers—was reassuring to us. It was good to know that such a school exists. The director was also reassuring in her advice.

"These are the worst years," she told us. "Things will get easier as Noah gets older. Growth is optimum even in the abnormal. Even though sometimes for your own good you have to remember that Noah isn't a normal child. And just forget about him, ignore him; he won't have the normal reactions. So don't worry about it."

I still have California on my mind for the winter. And it is comforting to know that we might have a possible future in Connecticut. Just driving there, the golden-auburn trees made one feel there might be autumnal solutions for Noah. But we still have to look for some spring ones. I want to do *now* what can be done *now*.

October 19, 1970

After Noah kept us up again for the fifth straight night, we changed his and Karl's rooms. I think we'll hear him less from across the corridor than from next door. Anyway it's worth trying.

October 20, 1970

We should have switched the rooms long ago. We slept the better for it.

I've been doing some more reading on autistic children. It seems to me there is a gulf between parents of autistic children and most professionals in the field—and that gulf is guilt. We're wary of assigning it; psychologists and psychiatrists and educators are looking to assign it. And I've decided that from now on I'm going to listen only to the consumers in the field, the parents, not the professionals with their own wares to sell. At the same time, I can't get too locked in with other parents. There is also the danger of becoming a member of an elitist club all wrapped up in a single noble cause. One of the results of my life may be a dedication to children like Noah, but it will not be its purpose.

October 21, 1970

A letter came asking me to sign a statement accepting complicity with the Vietnam war draft dodgers. I've signed enough such statements in the past, but now I'm hesitant. It's not that I'm afraid to go to jail, I'm afraid of the lurch it would leave Foumi and Karl in with Noah if I were to go.

California is set in my mind; now I only have to implement it. The most difficult detail of all is what to do with our cat, Brodsky. He's not like a house; we just can't leave him standing here.

October 22, 1970

I spoke with a chemist who told me he knows what might be wrong with Noah: Noah's been slowly poisoned all his life. He talked about sequestering agents that draw off the vital minerals, and how the fluoride in our water is a sequestering agent. I told him we have no fluoride in our water supply. He went on to explain how the world has been going nuts since 1960, when 600 food additives were let loose by the Federal Drug Administration, and I went on listening to him, even though he may be a quack. I'll listen to anybody. Especially since everybody seems to know so little.

Still thank God for Foumi's reality detector. I am psychogenic-prone, being of Jewish literary bent. It is Foumi who has steered us onto the biochemical and behavioristic roads. But none of these roads, I fear, will really ever get us out of the forest we're in with Noah. All there are now, I think, are mopping-up operations.

But the vitamin doctor called and told us he finally has some B-15, the vitamin the Russians have been using to stimulate speech.

October 23, 1970

I had a chat with an advertising copywriter I know who has a hydrocephalic (water-on-the-brain) kid about Noah's age. His boy talks but is not social. And he and his wife have been at such wit's ends that they even separated for a month. What was valuable to me as I listened to the outpouring of his whole story was the ad he had written to get some help in the house. It went something like this: "Who would like to help a beautiful, bright, handicapped four-year-old to learn to walk and talk? Full/part-time. Flexible hours. Nurse/therapist or high-school or college trainee will also be considered."

"Believe it or not," he said, "I put all my professional

training into writing that ad. I realized I would have to find highly motivated people. And it was the only way." He put the ad in a local shopper's guide and got twenty-six responses, out of which they found a half-dozen people to interview and choose from.

He also told me, in passing, that a doctor's note saying such help was necessary would make the salaries paid tax-deductible. Something to remember.

The director of the school in Connecticut also called. She was eager to have us bring Noah there on the seventeenth of November, when both the school's psychiatrist and speech therapist would be there, ready to look him over.

Connecticut is near and cold. California is far away and smoggy. But it is just as easy to consider moving to California as to Connecticut.

At first I thought that psychologists were more important than psychiatrists when it came to offering help to Noah. Now I'm beginning to think that educators are more important than the psychologists in actually improving his condition.

October 24, 1970

I read a book about the Chicago trials, and I thought of Noah. I'm not sure I'm for revolution anymore, nor that I can afford to be. If the pram in the hallway is the enemy of art, then the special child in the playroom is the enemy of revolutionary change. What happens to kids like Noah during a revolution? Even if the system is responsible for children like Noah in certain ways (because of restrictive abortion laws, because of a failure to enact birth-control legislation), ironically, as long as there are children like Noah, it cannot be stopped completely. To bring the system to a halt would require violence. And the first victims of any violence, the first to fall in any sort of a critical standstill, are the old, the sick, the handicapped, and the children. And a Noah fits three of those four categories.

October 25, 1970

Almost every night after dinner I wrestle with Karl on the rug. I never win; I always feign defeat, until I *cheat* my way off my back with "no-fair" tickling, and we end up in an orgy of laughing that we call a tie. Meanwhile Noah bounces on the couch or wraps himself around a pillow, wrestling a phantom opponent of his own.

Lately, Noah has become fascinated with running water. First it was from the taps alone, but now a flushing toilet really pleases him. He has been on B-15 just two days, but Foumi thinks she heard him say "Cut the cake" at dinner tonight. And I thought I heard him say "Go upstairs" just after I had urged him to do so in those very words before his bedtime.

October 27, 1970

The director of Noah's school had called, saying that his teacher wanted us to get him there earlier. Though his school starts at nine, I usually bring him there at about nine-thirty. That's because we like to have him breakfast after us. If Noah sees any bread on the table, he won't eat anything else. I explained that to Noah's teacher this morning. I also explained that Noah required time in the morning to dally hopefully in the john. But she said she still would like us to get him to school on time, that it would be good to have him start his class time with his classmates. So we'll make an effort.

October 28, 1970

Because of my parents' diabetic past and my own history of a hyperactive thyroid, I thought it might be useful to have Noah tested for hyperglycemia. I called our vitamin psychiatrist and asked him about it. He said he felt Noah was too young to be tested (a five-hour glucose-tolerance test) and too young to be treated (with adrenal cortex) for hyperglycemia. He suggested that we just keep on with the megavitamins, give them a chance for several years.

But I also spoke with an old college classmate who has worked as a principal in special schools. He told me: "Don't try anything for more than a year. If you're not getting results, no matter what anyone advises you, quit and try something else."

October 30, 1970

I got Noah to school on time. The teachers were waiting, Halloween masks on their faces; and I think I spotted a slightly bewildered, slightly bemused expression in Noah's eyes.

October 31, 1970

Foumi constantly had to change Noah today, and said he was just too much for her, more than she could handle, that we'd have to put him away.

And UCLA isn't promising anything. Noah will have to be examined, evaluated, and then they'll decide what to do with him. We'll go out to LA anyway. What do we have to lose?

Last night was a bad night. The cares of the day had piled in on Foumi: Karl sliding in sand piles, dirtying his clothes constantly. Noah his usual un-toilet-trained self. People dropping in unexpectedly in the early evening. And then the avalanche excitement of Halloween tumbling in with the noisy parade of kids at the door trick-or-treating. By bedtime she was done in, sobbing tiredly, uncontrollably, not even quite knowing why. Finally the sniveling stopped and she slept.

And then I got up at midnight and decided to check Noah. He was dry. I took him to the bathroom. He began to yell and howl. So the night wore on, with Foumi up and sobbing again.

And this morning, red-eyed, she was arguing that we would have to put Noah in an institution soon. She pointed out that our cat, Brodsky, operates on a much higher level than our son; that at least he knows not only how to communicate his vital needs but also how to attend to them; that for the sake of our own survival we have to get a respite from the problems of Noah; that Noah is simply becoming too much and that we must remember that three is a bigger number than one.

All this I know. Our lives must come first. Yet institutions mean cold, slow death to me, a surrender of a life to an organism that does not really care. Hospitals just as surely as they can heal and enhance life can wound and ultimately destroy it.

A lovely day of golden leaves falling. And Karl is thriving on a street life for the first time, spending almost every possible hour down on the block. (I can remember, in the marrow of my bones, how I discovered the society of the street I lived on too.) I do not relish the idea of uprooting him for the sake of Noah.

Foumi and I still talk about putting Noah in an institution. But I do recall the Connecticut lady said: "Things will get better, not worse." And I pray she's right.

Karl's aunt sent him an electric auto-racing set. We put up the tracks this evening, and he and I had a great time with it. But when I called his aunt and asked Karl to come to the phone to thank her, he refused to do so. Figure out kids—even allegedly normal ones.

I talked to the Connecticut lady again this morning. Once more she spoke of the need for parents of autistic children to compartmentalize their lives, not to allow their lives to revolve completely about the troubled child, indeed, to realize how necessary it is to cut the child completely out of certain activities.

Having the school, she said, for example, has helped her

to compartmentalize her life. She and her husband have been able to get away on vacations because they could get married couples who teach at the school to house- and autistic-child-sit. ("Without joy, how can you live?" she said. "You have to go away and forget once in a while about your problem, and do things with people who don't even know you have an autistic child.") And she spoke of the difficulty involved with a sibling, how one had to be fair to the other child too.

I voiced some of my complaints about our situation and then stopped short. I realized how absurd it was to cry on her telephone shoulder. But again she wanted to remind me that the worst was probably over, that things get better as the child gets older: he calms down and is more controllable.

But tell it to Foumi, who faces the daily grind of reality with Noah. Again she is saying she can't go on, that Noah is too much, that she doesn't see the point in throwing her life away for him.

I called the fellow townsman whose daughter is in an institution. "You'd better be ready to put the kid in an institution," he said, "before you have to put your wife in one."

It won't be that easy to get Noah into a good place, I gather. One has to pull strings, offer quids for quos. I would certainly be willing to do so. What other choice does one have?

November 13, 1970

Last Thursday I flew to California and met Dr. Lovaas at UCLA. He said they would accept Noah for therapy three times a week, for one-hour sessions in the afternoon. He also would be sending a student out to our house once we got there. And he told me of two nursery schools Noah might attend while there. I left his office in high spirits. But on Saturday morning I breakfasted with the father of a twelve-year-old autistic child who had been through the UCLA treatment and had gotten "a little but not much out of it." The father, however, still seemed to think UCLA was worth a try. His son, though, is not as yet toilet-trained. Which struck me as a grim prospect. I asked him what he was trying to do for the kid now. "I'm an accountant," he said, "so I'm trying to lay in money for his future. That's the best thing I can do."

Lovaas himself told me: "I promise no miracles, I hold out little hope. A lot will depend upon the ability of you and your wife to learn the therapies. Because if the treatments are not kept up, no matter what advances your boy makes, he will eventually backslide."

As usual, the best part of my trip was the return: Karl running to the door somehow seeming inches taller than I remembered him; Noah, though yelping and bouncing, still a beautiful sight to behold; and Foumi, the last to come in view, wiping her hands on her apron, looking truly lovely as I take her in my arms.

November 14, 1970

The social worker at County Health whom I've been in touch with called. She said there was only one institution she could possibly get Noah into in the near future. She told me the place. But that's the place where my fellow townsman had had his daughter. And he told me that on weekend visits he would note bruise marks on his daughter. I told the social worker to forget about a state institution for the time being.

A water main broke on the block. So Karl and the kids were sailing boats down the instant stream. Three times he came into the house all soaked, changed, and then charged out onto the street again. All day he was out there sailing pirate ships with prows of Styrofoam packing, leaves for sails, and ice-cream sticks for masts, down the gutter river.

Meanwhile, Noah was in the house, singing the song of his babble and endlessly rocking. My mother-in-law thinks he now makes his inexpressive sounds better because of the B-15.

A newlywed friend and his wife who is a speech specialist were up to see us last night. She thought that Noah might eventually be taught speech. I'm not that sure. Meanwhile they seem to have settled into their marriage. They wonder about having kids, though. She's worked with autistic children and knows all the dangers.

We went to Connecticut. Again I was impressed with the facilities of the school. They even have a gym where motor problems can be dealt with. We watched the gym teacher roll a ball back and forth to a kid who couldn't concentrate because he has peripheral vision. So like a horse that tends to run wide, they had him in blinders, trying to focus his vision straight ahead.

A psychiatrist and a speech therapist observed Noah. They seemed to think he was not too badly off "in a comparative sense." Compared to what? I asked. Compared to what he could be, I was told.

November 19, 1970

A resident school in Pennsylvania that I had written to for an application sent one in the mail. I thought that if they could cope with Noah, that might be the place for him. My thinking was academic. They want over $12,000 a year for openers.

November 20, 1970

I took Karl to the dentist for the first time, and he behaved admirably. We don't know what to do about Noah's teeth. They must be a mess from all of his grinding. But if we can't get him to open his mouth to brush his teeth, how can a dentist work on him?

November 21, 1970

We had another conference with Noah's teacher. She began by saying that she was applying a form of operant conditioning, using pretzels as rewards. She and her aide give the reward whenever he obeys a command such as "Stand up." And whenever he disobeys, they punish him. For example, if he crumples and picks at his sandwich at lunch, they throw it out. As a result, he has become much better at eating his sandwich by taking normal bites. He has also improved at taking off his coat and hanging it up and at pulling up his pants after going to the toilet.

The regime of the school is devoted to trying to give the children a practical and busy day. In the morning they are asked to take off their coats and push their chairs to the table. Then they go to the toilet. From 9:20 to 10:00 the teacher usually works with Noah on a one-to-one basis. Lately she has been working with a cup and spoon, asking Noah to give her the one or the other. When he gives her the cup, she rewards with a half-swallow of juice; when he gives her the spoon on command, he gets a piece of pretzel. And the idea, of course, is that he eventually does the command and is unmindful of the reward. If he pees on the floor, the teacher says, she makes no big deal of it. Mostly she believes in rewards rather than punishments. Ten o'clock is snacktime, a cheese or graham cracker and some juice. Toilet again. 10:20 to 10:35 is circle time. They sing songs which try to teach them their names, the parts of their bodies, concepts such as up and down. The teacher believes the children learn better from each other than from a teacher.

There are five children in Noah's group. Three other brain-damaged and/or autistic young boys and a mongoloid girl. She's by far the most advanced in the class. Group activity begins at 10:35. The youngsters finger-paint, which Noah loves, or use plastic glue, which he also digs. Or bake a pudding or pie that they will eat in the afternoon. The teacher tries to keep the play constructive. For example, if Noah in the first period goes to the sandbox, he cannot merely run sand through his fingers. He must fill or empty a pail. And the approbation he enjoys most is not a hug or a kiss but an applauding: "Yea Noah!" Noah will get on a bike and pedal a few turns toward a pretzel. (Indeed, it was funny to watch Noah frisk the apron pockets of both his teacher and her aide before we left.) At eleven o'clock they put on their coats and go out to play on the swings. Lunch is at 11:30, and afterward is tooth-brushing. It's as hard for them as it is for us to get Noah to brush his teeth, but at least he opens his mouth on the command in school now. Next, wash-up. And then each child brings his cot to his place—without getting a reward at this point. Noah usually sleeps from 12:15 to 1:15, and he tantrums there as he does at home when he is awakened; 1:15 is toilet time again, and the remaining time is a free activity.

The main thing, the teacher says, is to be consistent. Now they are trying to teach the children the nursery-school way of putting on their coats. Noah manages one sleeve before losing interest. But his interest span, she notes, has lengthened. He can sit for fifteen minutes during the one-to-one session, whereas in the past he would start wandering off after fifteen seconds.

Last night I reported all this to Foumi. She was pleased. We both wonder whether it is the "primitive" operant conditioning or the vitamins that are responsible for the changes; meanwhile, we'll continue with both.

November 23, 1970

Solutions pose problems. We planned to leave for California next week to get Noah, into the operant conditioning program at UCLA. But yesterday the new acting director of Noah's school told me that there might not be a place for Noah upon our return, that another child on the waiting list would assume his place. She did assure me, though, that Noah would have an excellent chance of getting into the school in the fall again, that as a former student he would be given priority. But that still leaves us facing a hurdle when we return. We may have less than we started out with. I feel as I did in the army: one never knows when one is transferring into a worse outfit, into a lousier theatre.

As for California we will apartment-hotel it for December. And then perhaps rent a house for three months. I do think at this point we'll be staying there until the end of March. It will be bad for Karl to be so dislocated; it will be good for Noah since he'll get more of the conditioning there and he'll miss less schooling when he gets back here, just two or three months. I feel I must make a different choice about what is best for either child. It is a choice I do not want to make. Because either way Noah or Karl comes out a loser.

November 25, 1970

Yesterday a friend saw Noah for the first time in months. He said Noah's attention span seems to have increased.

But my hopes are dim concerning Noah's future in the long run. If there are cures to be found, they will not apply to him. We must just find, I feel, a place that will teach us how to make do with him as best we can.

. I should feel more optimistic, I know. But Noah brings every dream crashing down to earth, pinpricks every fantasy balloon—even those dreams and fantasies about him.

November 26, 1970

We aren't sure the apartment hotel in Los Angeles will allow us to have a cat. So we've been wondering what to do about Brodsky, discussing the problem endlessly. I know we'll finally take him with us anyway. We have no choice. We've had him as long as we've been married.

November 28, 1970

It's getting painful to watch children grow past Noah. This afternoon we dined with some friends whose two-year-old son joined—or followed after—Karl and his older brother in play, while Noah just sat on the couch or in the corner, addressing his fingers and grinding his teeth.

The same thing happened Thanksgiving Day. Other friends were over with their three kids. Their baby girl, a little thing, now talks, while Noah remains a baby.

November 29, 1970

I've leafed through three books, chronicles by parents of severely disturbed or brain-damaged children. None of them palpitated with truth for me. The parents didn't burn with enough anger; they were all too damned heroic for me. Because one must be angry about all of the technology and all of the science that does not go into researching what the hell is wrong with a Noah. And as the parent of an autistic child, one is more ridiculous than heroic—like a sludging, sloshing infantry soldier in a nuclear age.

Indeed, the more I read about such children, the more I'm convinced, unfortunately, that only money can solve most of the problems of having a child like Noah. That's the damned truth of it. The more money I have, the less of a problem Noah becomes—I can hire out the problem to others. Have a crazy kid and get to understand the gut meaning of a society.

I had lunch with a divorced concert pianist today who told me how much he missed the sound of children, and I was telling Foumi about it at dinner. "Let him have Noah for one night and see how much he misses the sound of children," she said. Karl, sitting at the table, put down his fork and looked up with wide imploring eyes: "Please don't give Noah away," he said. Foumi and I tried to keep talking, but we couldn't. And looked away. . . .

Packing day. Foumi manages somehow. And even I do my small share. We wondered about our cat, Brodsky. Our next-door neighbor volunteered to take care of him. But then we decided that leaving him next door might be too dangerous, too confusing. We could see him freezing on our steps all winter long. So we're taking him with us.

But the big event for me today came this afternoon, when I picked up Noah at his school. He mumbled a greeting to me: "Daddy."

Our fifth day in southern California, and we're full of many impressions and a great deal of thirst. The dry climate gets to one. We're living in an apartment hotel. It is very convenient, the kitchen is almost a joy, and there is little cleaning for Foumi.

I called Dr. Lovaas, but he was gone for the weekend. Meanwhile we visited two special schools that Noah might attend while we're here, and we'll decide on one of them.

At the moment, Noah is poking his foot along the pile rug as if it were surf he was dipping into. His head moves from side to side in a rolling motion, and his arms beat against the air—a weird swimmer in an alien element.

December 7, 1970

The city of Los Angeles shrinks each day; the more I drive, the more I get the feel of its sprawl. It's not at all unlike the Brooklyn I grew up in: a bunch of disparate neighborhoods each with its own main street. Except that in the Brooklyn I knew, trolleys rattled over cobblestoned avenues instead of Mercedes humming down palm-tree-lined boulevards. The few people we've run into here all have been relaxed and informal, yet also seemed lonely and transient. No wonder: the winds of divorce are everywhere. The hotel handyman, the housekeeper, the chambermaid, are all either divorced or involved in second marriages. Los Angeles also strikes me as a difficult place to meet new people. The swinging life here, I'm sure, has moments which hang very heavily.

But Noah seems to like it here. He sleeps well, tantrums little, and seems genuinely content. It is amazing how little I am willing to settle for, the longer we live with Noah and his problems. The simplest step of progression in any direction gives me the greatest feelings of satisfaction.

Now he is bouncing about, babbling to his fingers, having one of those uncontrollable moments of literally boundless enthusiasm that are his trademark. And Karl is following Noah around, imitating him, jumping as he does, announcing: "Now there is two Noahs in the family."

December 9, 1970

We took Noah over to UCLA to be videotaped. He was placed in an empty room except for a table full of toys. From another room behind a two-way glass mirror he was recorded by a camera and monitored for sounds. For the first ten minutes he was left in the room to do as he wished by himself: Noah did nothing except for his usual babble song and jumping dance. For the next ten minutes a student entered the room with a chair and sat there quietly, making no effort at all to involve Noah. Except for a moment or two, Noah barely noticed him. For the last ten minutes, at one-minute intervals, the student actively tried to interest him in various toys. Noah could scarcely have cared less.

Afterward I spoke to Lovaas in his office. He told me the purpose of the videotaping and monitoring was to establish a "baseline" on Noah's usual pattern of behavioral responses—or lack of responses—to outside stimuli. Also, hopefully, the videotape could serve as a dramatic "before" to be contrasted with the "after" picture. But again he warned me that an autistic or schizophrenic child who undergoes behavior therapy will usually not end up anywhere near normal, that his progress at best can be compared to climbing the first step of a ten-step ladder. The goals would be to suppress Noah's self-stimulation—

his senselessly repetitive motor acts which block out perceptions of the outside world and therefore impede learning; to teach him some elementary forms of language that he can use to express demands; to generally make him easier to live with at home by making his conduct more acceptable on a minimal social level.

Dr. Lovaas also reminded me that the treatment might sometimes call for the use of adverse stimuli such as spanking, slapping, weak electrical charges, and food deprivation as well as the use of rewards—or reinforcers—such as candy and potato chips. And I signed a release granting my permission.

We discussed the difference between psychogenic therapy and behavior therapy. "Simple," said Lovaas. "Behavior therapy proceeds independent of etiology. A treatment based on etiology has to rest on very shaky grounds since we do not know exactly why these children become as they are. So in the absence of such information it seems pointless to me to implicate parents and make them feel guilty, which is at the basis of the psychogenic approach."

I cracked a weak joke: "Every time somebody strikes Noah, I'm going to feel guilty."

Lovaas put his hand on my shoulder and looked me straight in the eye: "Look, the little that we can do is the only form of treatment which has scientifically demonstrated effectiveness. Besides"—he laughed—"nobody is going to bat your kid around. Don't worry about it." He then bent over, picked up Noah, who had been prancing about his office, began to jiggle him playfully on his knee, and laughing affectionately, buried his blond Norwegian head into Noah's giggling face.

Noah started nursery school this morning. And I'm not sure we made the right choice. They didn't seem exactly one-hundred-percent prepared for him, lacking proper potty facilities on the premises. He also had his first operant-conditioning session.

Foumi and I sit in a control booth like radio-network vice-presidents. The treatment room is a mini-studio: two chairs, a table ledge with a cluster of keys, a model car, a bag of Fritos on top of it, and a two-way mirror. From behind the mirror we observe. Laura, one of the two therapists who will work with Noah, walks in with him. She sits Noah down facing her. She cracks the Fritos into little pieces and arranges them beside her. Then she begins: "Noah, look at me." Each time he does so, or almost does so, she rewards him with a sliver of a chip, tufts his hair, and says: "Good boy." Now she moves on, using the "Look at me" as a point of return and reward, asking him to clap his hands just as she is clapping hers: "Noah, do this." Once he does so, and is lavishly praised and rewarded. But the other attempts fail. Laura returns to: "Look at me, Noah." When his attention wanders, when he begins to gleefully self-stim, getting lost in observing his fingers dance erratically, she rebukes him with a sharp, "Noah!" Now she lifts her hand: "Noah, do this." And once or twice he does, tentatively, but then ignores the rest of the commands. Again: "Look at me, Noah," the hair rub, the "good boy, Noah." Laura turns to the cluster of keys: "Give them to me, Noah." He does so: the "good boy," the hair rub, the Frito. Sometimes on the command Noah's hand absently wanders over to the object, the car or the keys she is asking for. Other times with great alacrity the task is dispatched. Now Noah suddenly acts as if he's very sleepy. He starts to tantrum. Laura looks away, does not comfort him, refuses to get involved with him. The tantrum passes, the sleepiness disappears, the tasks continue. Laura addresses us through the mirror: "You must never let him determine when you can stop working with him. The last thing he does must always be the obeying of a command—even if it's just a simple: 'Look at me.' Because otherwise, he'll think he can get out of doing anything by having a tantrum or acting sleepy or just self-stimming in general."

Afterward we see Lovaas. He tells us that Laura and Meredith, the other girl who will work with Noah, are two of his very best therapists. Meanwhile, I notice the battery-charged shocker, like a cattle prodder, on Lovaas' desk. I have heard of it, but still, seeing it is disconcerting. I wonder if it will be used on Noah. Just then a tired Noah wanders into the office. Lovaas bends down, placing his own knees on the floor, to tie Noah's trailing shoelaces. The gesture endears him to me enormously, counteracting the sting at the sight of the shocker.

December 12, 1970
Karl likes his school, but I kept him out of class yesterday so he could watch a friend of mine direct a TV Western on the back lot of Universal. Karl held a real gun for the first time, poked into the covered wagons and stagecoaches, and saw "real movie horses."

December 18, 1970

If until now at Noah's sessions I've been viewing my child as a dog getting trained, yesterday I saw him as a monkey in an experiment. Laura worked with Noah at a machine made of beaverboard and controlled by a great many spaghetti wires and toggle switches and hooked into a tape recorder. A visual image (a bulb lighting) or an audio signal (a beep) are given to Noah. If he responds to either, by touching a lever within a given number of seconds, he is rewarded with a Frito. In this way they hope to discover which sort of stimulus Noah might be more responsive to—audio or visual—or if he is more responsive to both simultaneously than to each separately.

December 19, 1970

Foumi feels we should stay in the hotel. Karl likes his school, his class, and there is an advantage to a small apartment we never figured on: Karl need never feel neglected, no matter how much attention we tend to give Noah, because he is never that far from the center of attention.

But I like space. And being boxed in with Noah lately, I find that he wears on me more, his teeth-grinding and soprano whining cutting through the tattered endings of my nerves.

December 24, 1970

At home now Noah's been playing with his Busy Box, moving the car back and forth, like a one-year-old. At UCLA they've been working on getting him to clap his hands, raise them, and touch his head with them on cue.

Mostly, though, he seems to me to be crying in protest. But his therapists, Laura, loving yet firm, and Meredith, who seems to exude the spirit of an Israeli woman army officer, have monumental patience. Any progress with Noah, they tell us, will come slowly, agonizingly so. We should expect eye droplets and thimblefuls, not buckets full of rain, to mark the changes of his climate.

A girl came to see us, the older sister of an autistic boy. She was looking for some baby-sitting jobs over the holidays. Whether we can use her or not I don't know, but I was pleased to see that she had come through her side of that sibling experience quite well. In her big granny glasses, her straight hair, her simple long gown, she looked like any other hippie with a normal kid brother.

December 26, 1970

Foumi has noted that Noah has all but stopped talking in California. But Dr. Lovaas said his speech was probably gradually fading out anyway. And I recall the Connecticut lady pointing out that as children like Noah move forward in one area, they generally fall back in another. I don't know what area he is quite progressing in at the moment, but I do feel he is more contented out here. And just as important, Foumi is more hopeful, so she's in better spirits.

In the long run I've come to be less sanguine. Because what we're working toward ideally is ten percent of a normal human being, a child we can cope with about the house, whom we can keep at home as long as possible. If at this stage of the game Brodsky, our cat, functions more intelligently than Noah, it is a fact I have grown to accept. If most of operant conditioning is nothing less than old-fashioned dog training, it is something I do not scoff at. I must admit, though, that on the rare occasions Noah is struck during a treatment, I flinch and clench my fists. Even though he is no ordinary child, he is my child, and I entertain the ordinary feelings of parental outrage. But then I remind myself that what love and affection can't always accomplish, perhaps a little fear and duress can.

Karl was delighted with his Christmas in the sun. Especially the Instamatic camera we gave him. He's been snapping pictures all day, popping flash bulbs all evening. And before he went to bed tonight he asked me why we had also given him a magic box and paper balloons as gifts. I explained that when I was a boy I liked the magic box and Foumi as a girl enjoyed playing with balloons. Somehow it all didn't get through clearly to him: "Do I have to give my toys to my children when I grow up?" he asked.

Epistemology and nomenclature fascinate a child. Karl has frequently asked me questions such as: "What if all the children were called adults, and all the adults were called children?" And I think too many psychiatrists and psychologists tend to get lost in the allure of the same kinderspiel.

December 28, 1970

We went to a party in Venice at a friend of a friend's house. The hostess's son was once diagnosed as autistic. He did not speak until he was past five, and was in diapers until he was six. Now he goes to an ordinary junior high school. He still seems a little strange; he cannot stop an activity once he is involved in it; his room is a mess. But obviously he functions on what one is tempted to call an idiosyncratically normal creative level. He draws cartoon strips, for example.

We asked the mother what she had done.

She has blocked out most of the hard years. But she does recall: "I refused to accept any diagnosis—and I got them all; I insisted that he be placed in a regular school; I worked with him constantly myself—teaching, teaching, teaching him endlessly; and the only medication I gave him was Deanor."

Oh, that Noah could turn out half as well.

December 30, 1970

I was hugging and kissing Noah in bed when I suddenly stopped: I realized I have to contain myself a bit when it comes to giving him affection gratuitously, that it would be almost self defeating to do so. This operant conditioning is pretty hard on me in that respect.

January 4, 1971

We moved on New Year's Day. Karl is pleased with the house we rented because it's in the same school district as the hotel, so he doesn't have to change schools. Noah is delighted with the panoramic views provided by our floor-to-ceiling windows. We're keeping him out of school for the moment.

This morning I tried to do a little operant conditioning on him for the first time. It was a frustrating experience; I was often tempted to haul off and sock him. At this point Noah will immediately put his hands over his head in an attempt to please and get an immediate reward. But he won't clap his hands for anything. Or differentiate between commands. At every command he simply puts his hand over his head. This was comic but heartbreaking, the stuff of Beckettian comedy—and, of course, our own small human tragedy.

The purpose of these command exercises is to teach Noah how to imitate, the first steps in any learning process, the steps he has so far refused to take. But as I put him through these paces I thought again of placing him in an institution. Perhaps it is better to live at a remove from one's most personal problems.

January 5, 1971

Noah is in bed yelling "Oh gees" of protest. He knows he's done something wrong and that we don't feel too warmly toward him. Three times in less than two hours he has b.m.'ed in his diapers.

January 6, 1971

I love to walk Karl to school each morning. We amble along in easy camaraderie. This morning we were speaking of money, his lunch money. "If I drop my money into dirt," he asked, "does that mean I have a dirty lunch?"

January 7, 1971

Foumi's first day as a therapist—or a therapist in training. She went into the booth with Noah, and Meredith stayed there instructing her, giving her pointers. It seemed to go quite well. Noah cried a little, but Foumi "worked

137

through the crying," getting him to respond tolerably well to her commands. Meredith commended her, and she came away feeling proud and hopeful—until she began to wonder whether the commendation wasn't a form of operant conditioning itself.

I talked with Lovaas again. He told me that the difficulty with a Noah is getting him to want something badly enough, or to be afraid of something badly enough, to respond to either fulfillment of the desire or an avoidance of that which is distasteful. Then when the action becomes rote, the reward or the punishment can be phased out. "But the trouble with Noah is, we really still can't get a good hook into him," he said. "Noah will expend a single calorie in situations the average person or child will expend ten times as much. He just doesn't have any energy levels behind his likes and dislikes."

January 9, 1971

Laura observed Foumi today as she tried to put Noah through his paces. And Laura duly commended her, even though it was a difficult session. For the most part, Noah refused to look at the object he was supposed to pick up, his hand absently somehow always groping or gliding toward it. I doubt if he was burning even half a calorie in the performance of the task.

January 10, 1971

I still love the mornings in California, the sun, the autumnal chill, as I walk Karl to school, him loping behind me, mimicking adult thoughts, trying on mature poses in his childish way. And after I deposit him at his schoolroom door and meander back through the neat jungle-green streets, a creative pause comes over me, ideas rush in, and I feel as if I were truly young and vibrantly alive and earnestly questing to be an artist again. But then as the day wears on full of Noah details, and the logistics of transportation and household chores, I wonder again when my life will really begin, when I will ever be attending primarily to my own things.

January 11, 1971

For the past several days Noah has "self-stimmed" to an unusual degree before going to sleep. The theory behind "self-stimulation," or the repetition of stereotyped behavior, the constant repeating of the same simple action, such as jumping or head-shaking or finger-talking, is that for an organism to stay alive it must be stimulated. And if it doesn't receive stimulation from the outside world, it stimulates itself. And yet by the same destructive token, while it is stimulating itself it cannot receive stimulation from the outside world. It's all a vicious circle a child like Noah can't break out of.

If one has a child like Noah, one needs money. In order to get enough money, one must have the time and the energy to work. But a child like Noah drains away one's energy, takes away one's time. There is simply no way out.

I must confess something: sometimes I hope Noah gets sick and dies painlessly.

January 12, 1971

Foumi's back has been bothering her, and we went to see a chiropractor about it. He was taken with Noah,

139

asked us all about him, and offered to treat him free of charge. But treat him for what?

We're putting Noah into another school. It has only autistic children. We visited there this afternoon. All of the students, varying in age from seven to fourteen, look like Noahs at further stages of development.

Yesterday one boy was waiting to go home. And finally he blurted out: "Mama coming." One could see how much energy and intense concentration it had taken him to work up to the moment. Perhaps someday Noah will be able to speak like that.

January 13, 1971

A friend called from New York, asking, among other things, about Noah and how he was coming along. Confronted with that question, I suddenly had to take stock and answer that "he is coming along." Noah's attention span seems to have increased, he is much quicker to obey simple commands. I can get him to come to me when I call him, to sit down, to stand up, to pull down and pull up his pants. Except for nocturnal emissions and bowel movements, he goes to the bathroom when we bring him there. All of his motions, though, remain halfhearted and uncommitted. And he tends to repeat the last-learned action rather than the appropriate one. He is classically funny in that way. But it is also almost painful to watch him strain toward any new learning, even though it is rewarding to see it finally emerge. For it means there will never be one big gestalt of a miracle—one's secret dream, one's treasured notion—a dramatic breakthrough with an organ chord sting. Rather each step of his development will be like a long chapter in a plodding, earnest multi-paged novel.

I continue to ration my love to Noah—or my expression of it. I no longer indulge in arbitrary huggings. And perhaps I'm displacing this need by giving more overt affection to Karl. Yesterday I took him to the library with me. The librarian asked him, as she noticed me taking out a book for him on my card, if he wanted a card of his own. All he would have to do, she said, was know how to write his own name. He burst into tears, embarrassed by the fact that he wasn't certain he could write his own name. When we returned home, I made him first copy his name ten times and then write it another ten times without looking at it. He did so. And soon he was huggable and cuddly, intensely pleased with himself and pleased with the warmth of my tough hugs.

January 14, 1971

It occurs to me that though Noah is a "wild child" in that he tends to bring out the miracle worker in all of us, he is more an "idle child" in that he continually wanders about the house not doing a damn thing.

January 15, 1971

Karl knows how to break my heart. He was running a slight fever, so we put him to bed early tonight. And I lay down with him and we chatted about our lives, our family, and our family lives. Suddenly he asked me in a most plaintive way: "When Noah is trained, will he be able to play with me?" I choked and held back tears. Later I told Foumi the question and let her cry for both of us.

The chiropractor is treating Noah every day, coming to the house, trying to work his miracles. I know nothing about chiropractic as differentiated from fakery. I do know that he is a kind and sensitive man.

This morning I took a walk with Noah in the bright sun, and it felt like an eternally youthful sun, walking hand in hand with him, very father-and-son-ish, until I realized again that one of the sad things about a Noah is that one can never be warmed by the sense that one is helping to store away pleasant memories in a child.

The chiropractor continues to come daily. He may not have magic, but he certainly does have industry.

One of those lulu nights. As we prepared to go to bed, Karl rushed in with a nosebleed. Next Noah reeked of a b.m. We ministered and maided to both, and finally tried to sleep. But now Noah was up in full nocturnal concert. And on it went until dawn. If I ever dig in any place for any long period of time, I will have to soundproof his room. It's the only way we can survive. Without sleep we're not only physically beat but also mentally churlish, snapping at each other for the least little thing. It is as if love fatigues easily and requires tender nourishment and constant refreshment through rest and sleep.

January 22, 1971

Noah was sick all day, but now he seems to have recovered, whelping out his gleeful whees and whoops in strident tones like a crazed animal. On nights like this I wish he were a cat so we could put him out of the house. Instead, we'll put ourselves out of the house by going to a movie to preserve our sanity. Insanity—or whatever his brand of mental illness—is catching.

January 24, 1971

I napped this afternoon and woke up in the midst of the usual recurring dream. Noah suddenly and casually had begun to talk. And people looked at me and said: "What's all the hassle been about this kid, anyway?"

I alternately shiver and shudder, love and hate, my family. Especially Noah. To live with madness, one must love with madness.

January 25, 1971

I took Noah to the pediatrician. He had a slight ear infection. But the discovery of the fact did not resolve anything between me and Foumi. We've been going at it all day, having a real battle royal. This always happens when Noah is sick. The strain tells. One thing we did agree on, though, at the bitter height of our argument:

143

how absurd it would be for either of us to commit suicide because of Noah.

Foumi and I are still battling, but a bigger event has overtaken us. Noah started his new school in a small California Ginger Bread house. Classrooms forced into the mold of a structure not quite ready to accept them. A big fenced-in yard with swings and playground equipment.

His teacher, Mrs. Harris, called this afternoon with the news that Noah urinated standing up. Foumi and I ceased our fighting and embraced each other in celebration. Foumi feels that if not a miracle, at least the sign of a miracle, has occurred.

The teacher also reported his attention span was long and he was alert. A very good first day of school for Noah.

But on this bad day between me and Foumi—our fights can last a week, as Foumi is slow to anger but, once enraged, impossible to soothe—I began to think that just as an autistic child can be the cause of the breakup of a good marriage (or an otherwise good marriage), perhaps he can also be the reason for the perpetuation of an otherwise bad marriage.

January 28, 1971

Everyone wants a piece of Noah—like the Odd Man Out. And often, no matter how well-intentioned the people are, we have to expend energy rejecting their offers of "help." Because the "help" may not turn out to be very effective. I had to tell the chiropractor this afternoon that I think Noah has had enough adjustments for the moment. I said we were too busy, Noah's schedule was too full, and that we didn't want to impose on the chiropractor's time.

It was comparatively easy to ease him out. It was much more difficult to get rid of a student Lovaas had sent over to our house to help put Noah through his paces at home. In that case Noah's fate had to be tied into academic rigmarole. The student was arrogant, smug, seemed more inclined to punish Noah than to reward him. When I told him that I thought we could make do without him, he was crushed: "You don't understand," he said, "Noah is very important to me. He means six credits." Finally I had to prevail upon Lovaas, in his role of professor, to assign other "research projects" to the particular student.

And Lovaas is primarily involved in a research project on the utilization of conditioning techniques as therapeutic tools. But he himself is a virtuoso therapist. On the occasions he has "worked" with Noah he has been a marvel and a revelation to observe—always firm but affectionate, strong yet loving. He has been able to elicit responses out of Noah—the repetition of sounds, for example—that no one else can. His students—or disciples—are all stiff and derivative compared to him. For the tough-treatment approach obviously derives from a gentle-hearted man who can thus in a sense "play the patient" with the skill of a classically trained musician hip to all the joys of jazz improvisation.

January 29, 1971
Yesterday I went into the booth for the first time. And I was lavishly praised by Lovaas and Meredith and Laura for

the way I worked with Noah. But I suspect they were perhaps trying to operant-condition me.

January 31, 1971

Mrs. Harris, the teacher at Noah's school, tells me my son has been adapting very well. Yet as I watch Noah make his advances, his huge steps—such as simply responding to his name or "coming here" on signal—are infinitesimal. I realize that a dog in two nights at obedience school is still light-years ahead of my boy. And no matter how inured I've become as I watch the kids at his school, various Noahs jabbing the air grotesquely, picking lint meticulously, rocking wildly on the swings, I still have to turn away after a few seconds. I really can't quite yet accept myself as the father of a Noah. I just can't cast myself in that part—which is, of course, my role for life.

February 2, 1971

I drove Noah to school this morning again. He wandered around the schoolyard, a Lilliputian among Gullivers. But on the way to school he did not protest carrying his own lunchbox. I must remember to use more praise than criticism with him. I tend to overact—or to ego-react —with him. I forget that, with all of the infuriating wave-of-the-hand measure of energy—or lack of energy—he approaches any task with, he has been making gigantic baby-step strides. We now can get him to raise, clap, and stretch his hands up and down on cue. He'll also respond to "sit down," "stand up," and "pick this up." He protests against learning, but still lazily tries to please. And that's the important nub of it: he can learn.

I also noticed this morning that the halfhearted feeble gesture is a trademark of the autistic kid. The teacher had the children all sitting in a row on a bench. She threw a basketball to each of them. And asked each kid to throw it back. Some of the kids just pushed it lightly. Noah lifted himself off the bench as he push-threw it.

February 4, 1971

Noah's session was generally undistinguished. I worked with him under Meredith's supervision for most of the time. I could get him to do imitative behavior physically, but I couldn't do a thing with words. Meredith reminded me how much effort we'd had to expend to get him to clap his hands six weeks ago. One forgets the small triumphs so easily.

February 5, 1971

Lovaas worked with Noah. He got him to repeat simple respiratory sounds such as "ah" and "pip." He was certainly like the musician pushing his instrument by feel into new areas of expression. Usually he was gentle with Noah, but once when Noah reached out to take his reinforcer —or reward, the Frito—Lovaas slapped him down hard.

Another student is going to work with Noah in addition to the three sessions a week Noah has with Meredith and Laura. He's a kid named Tom who'll be concentrating on speech.

Noah has really caught on to the knack of urinating standing up. The only trouble is, he does not yet tell us when he is ready to perform that trick. So Foumi sometimes still has the feeling that her life is draining away in never-ending toilet changes. But generally we're pleased with his progress here, the climate—except for the smog—and the fact that Karl is happy. Each morning now a little Japanese boy who lives across the street and a blond Caucasian who lives next door call on him to walk to school. Karl has a life on the block, and that is all that concerns any six-year-old.

The earth shook this morning. At six o'clock it trembled us awake, and Foumi and I got out of bed and onto the floor. Karl came into our room: "What is it?" "An earthquake," we told him. "Oh," he said. "It's fun." He rubbed his eyes and returned to bed. Meanwhile, not even the great California earthquake of 1971 could get through to Noah. He slept through it all.

Noah did better today at UCLA as his sessions went on. First Laura worked with him. But he cried a lot, and it was obvious neither patient nor therapist was very much in the mood. Then I took a short fling and didn't do well. Next Meredith came on, and she had him pulling the string through block beads. Finally, Tom, the student who'll emphasize speech, worked softly and effectively, getting

Noah to imitate "ahs" and "mmms," if not quite on cue or too precisely, at least not too infrequently.

I love the vocabulary of the UCLA kids. It's almost as colorless and as unemotionally communicative as the jargon of the astronauts. Words and expressions like "extinguishing behavior" for putting a stop to conduct, "fading the prompt" for withdrawing a cue gradually, "reinforcer" for reward. And so on. But if it can get us to our moon, I'll gladly abide any linguistic crimes.

February 10, 1971

I had coffee this morning with the father of a thirteen-year-old boy in Noah's school. He told me his son still bed-wets and can never be relied on to communicate any of his toilet plans. So I worked doubly hard with Noah this afternoon. But even though I could get him to repeat my hand motions, he wouldn't do any talking at all.

February 18, 1971

We went up to San Francisco for a long holiday weekend, and had a great time visiting old friends there. Noah behaved famously, never b.m.'ed in his pants, and urinated only twice in the wrong place. But we've come home to discover that Brodsky, our cat, is dying. So a pall has descended over our house.

To further add to the gloom is the fact that yesterday's session at UCLA was utterly frustrating, a total washout. Noah seemed unable to learn the slightest amount because he was busy crying all hour long.

This morning, though, Mr. Harris told me that Noah

does have periods of imitating sounds, that he is young after all, that one can't expect too much of him at once. Again I'm confused. I read so much how important the four-to-six-years-of-age period is for speech development. Yet I'm also told that it is hard for the very young such as Noah to learn. Who to believe?

February 19, 1971

Brodsky had been sick for the past few weeks. Yesterday he could barely move. We brought his food and water near him. He wouldn't touch his food at all, barely drank the water, and seemed to put all of his energy into angry hisses. So last night I took him to the vet. This morning I called the animal hospital from my office and was told they were about to call me: "He passed away during the night." I called Foumi and said something like: "You know why I'm calling." And she began to cry. Then she asked if she should tell Karl. Last night Karl had sobbed when we warned him that Brodsky was sick and might die. Death is so hard for an adult to explain to a child, because I think a child understands it too well: he need not read John Donne to know instinctively that the death of any animal is a signal of his own eventual death as well.

Brodsky was a great symbol to Foumi and me. He was the *chochin mochi*, as the Japanese say, the bringer-of-us-together, in our marriage. I had taken him to the MacDowall Colony the summer Foumi and I met, and I half-intended to dump Brodsky on her and take off for France. Instead I waited for her to bring Brodsky back to the city, and we soon married, Brodsky occupying an important position in the mythology of the rest of our lives. We took him back to MacDowall the following summer, and to Maine, and to Canada, and to Japan, and now to California. I hope his death does not symbolize death in terms of our trip here.

I also hope his death does not symbolize the end of our dedication to Noah. For just as Karl identifies the death of Brodsky with his own eventual death, I think I have identified the fate of Brodsky with the destiny of Noah. They are both, after all, my pets—endearing helplessnesses, responsibilities without end.

February 21, 1971

I continue to think of Brodsky's death in all of its ramifications. Now that our family grouping has begun to wither away, I can see it for the first time continuing without Noah, just as it is continuing without Brodsky. Nowhere is it written that we all have to live together as long as each of us is alive. In fact, last night at dinner, while Noah slept and Karl asked questions, it seemed we were an entirely different family, an almost normal family.

But having a Noah, I realize, does give one an unusual perspective from which to watch a child's growth. While Noah remains forever a baby step away from infancy, I can see most dramatically whatever changes take place in Karl's development as he moves toward maturity. For example, I now notice, he likes to make up jokes, to be funny. Reminds me in ways I can't stand of someone else as a boy: myself.

February 22, 1971

I tried to work with Noah this evening in the dressing room off our bedroom, which is about the size of the booth at UCLA. I put two chairs in there, sat down in one, and placed Noah on the other opposite me. But he would not even repeat a simple "ah" sound. He refused, he rebelled, he cried and cried. It was enormously frustrating. I'm not sure now we can ever get Noah to talk. I'm not sure any effort on our part is worthwhile. The sonofabitch demands so much—and gives back so little.

February 25, 1971

These days I've been riding the emotional escalators again in regard to Noah. At the beginning of the week I dipped down. Noah wasn't responding to vocal imitations at all; one could work with him a whole hour and get barely a sound. But then Mrs. Harris, his teacher, has reminded me: "One can't expect miracles. There is no science. There is just each individual child." She tells me that he has been having good days at school, being attentive and alert.

And then at dinner tonight he spoke the first word he's spoken in California. I had gone to a Jewish delicatessen and brought back, among other things, bagels, which I know he loves. And Noah took one look at them and shouted: "Bagels!" How can I ever dream of letting go of a kid who has a one-word vocabulary consisting of "bagels." Now, if I can only get him to say "cream cheese and lox. . . ."

February 26, 1971

We took Noah to see a speech therapist, the brother of a friend. At first he admitted that he didn't know what to do with an autistic child. But then he met Noah and began to dream of playing God and curing him. He sat Noah in a room, and whenever Noah babbled, he babbled back at him. He's convinced that Noah is playing the private game of inventing his own language and does not talk in our language because he can get everything he wants in his own. We're convinced this speech therapist is much too Freudian in his approach, substituting literary analyses for practical solutions.

February 27, 1971

They "staffed" Noah at UCLA. At noon all of Lovaas' students gathered like an informal strike committee, paper-bag sandwich lunches before them, around a large conference table in a classroom to discuss Noah. Foumi and I testified like witnesses as to Noah's progress (great in visual imitations, minimal in speech therapies). Meredith and Laura and Tom issued their reports. A discussion followed as to what might be the next best step to help accelerate Noah's learning. Finally Lovaas suggested that Noah be put on a food-deprivation program of thirty-six hours to see how he would react, to show him dramatically that communications can bring him desired rewards.

Foumi and I agreed at the meeting. But then we've had second thoughts. Noah is young, he is not that withdrawn, thirty-six hours is a long time. And Lovaas himself pointed out that such a plan has only about a five-percent chance of being effective. So I called him this evening and said we'd like to cut down the length of the food-deprivation period to the omission of a breakfast or a lunch for openers.

Lovaas explained the need for a long-term trial. At the end of ten hours the child is dazed and dizzy; at the end of twenty hours he is searching for food; at the end of thirty-six hours he is desperate and will do anything to get food.

We finally worked out a compromise. Noah will be deprived of food—but not water or juice—from dinner one night to three-thirty the following afternoon. Which strikes me as a sufficiently long fast period. We'll do it next Wednesday.

February 28, 1971

Yesterday I was forty-three. What can one say about a man who is forty-three and still living? That he is still alive? That he feels young and old at the same time? That his memories are beginning to crowd in on his dreams? Or just: shit.

In a fit of family, I drove its members to the LA Museum of Natural History. Foumi enjoyed the pre-Columbian exhibition, Karl liked the dinosaurs, and Noah was interested only in the popcorn I kept pouring into his mouth.

March 3, 1971

The big fast day: Noah skipped breakfast, crying a little, as if he were sensing a lack, a missed beat, when I hustled him out of the house and on to school, but otherwise going without his usual food in a most submissive way. Picked him up at school before twelve—didn't want him to see the other children having their lunches—and brought him home, where he seemed happy enough. At three-thirty, over to UCLA. There they were all gathered in the observation room of the booth, Lovaas and his crew. (Lovaas: "This is an enormously rich country. Where else would eight adults gather to watch one four-year-old?") Meredith began to work with him, holding out spoonfuls of ice creams, pieces of bagel, as reinforcers. But Noah's reactions—or lack of them—were about the same as usual.

Then Lovaas asked if we would allow Noah to skip dinner and bring him back the next morning. "He's not hungry enough," he explained. And we agreed. So now it is nightfall, and Noah hasn't had a bite to eat all day. Nor has he drunk any of the liquids we've offered him. But amazingly, he isn't at all ill-humored, still jumping and giggling. Not even a lack of food really seems to reach him.

The purpose of the food-deprivation program, of course, is to find out exactly how much Noah will put out if he wants something badly enough. To place, as Lovaas intimated to me, "a firecracker up his ass." But at this point, knowing Noah, I suspect the firecracker will only sizzle.

March 4, 1971

The starvation diet—or whatever its euphemism—is a bust. We awoke this morning to hear Noah hacking, and when I looked in his crib I noted his sheets stained with yellow vomit-like mucus. It reminded me immediately of the stuff my father emitted before he died—the emissions of a stomach which is not functioning right at all.

We called Lovaas, and he called Meredith. She came to our house, looked at Noah quickly, and decided he couldn't be "worked with." We got some food into Noah

—but he refused to drink anything—and took him over to the pediatrician, where he received a clean bill of health. He explained that Noah had up-chucked bile because there was no food in his stomach for the enzymes and juices to work on.

Somebody should have warned us about that. Foumi knows starvation, terminal starvation, too keenly from the war; and the death of Brodsky is still too omnipresent for us not to be unduly sensitive.

So the past two days have been given again to learning there is no quick path. There is only patience. And even a behavioristic concept has to take into consideration the individual child and the instincts—or fears—of his particular parents. Foumi and I know that Noah has no deep reservoir of will, no great desire to live, and that there is always the danger that he could pass on in his own otherworldly way, not even with a whimper, but with a quiet unfocused smile.

March 5, 1971

At UCLA today Lovaas said he wanted to put Noah on another food-deprivation program to find out once and for all if food was a "successful hook." I said, "Let's just assume it isn't." He said he definitely wanted another try at it. I said, "No chance." He suggested putting Noah in the university hospital for a week while he was on food deprivation. I said, "Never." He sighed and said that we were trying to sabotage his efforts. I laughed and said, "Don't be so psychogenic." He said we were being overprotective parents. I said, "Once the odds have gone against you—as with a child like Noah—it's easy to be overprotective." And so we parried. At one point he said: "You worry too much about Noah. You should worry more about your other boy. Or maybe you should have another child. In that way you would worry less. The more children you have, the less you worry about." "But I have eleven children already. To have an autistic child," I said, quoting a Long Island mother of a child like Noah, "is to have ten children." He nodded slowly. Then he asked if his students might observe us as a family with Noah over an extended period such as all of Saturday. I said, "Certainly." And our discussion of the food-deprivation program ended with my inviting him and his wife for dinner on Saturday night.

March 7, 1971

We passed yesterday pleasantly, enjoying the camaraderie of the students as they "observed" us in shifts. Then the professor and his wife came for dinner. And it was good to see and talk with him away from his academic turf in the company of someone (his wife) who did not accept his every professional dictum as a tablet from Mt. Sinai. Indeed, Lovaas spoke of his boyhood in Norway, the war years he spent on a farm, his father, who was a journalist, his sister, who is a "kook," and of his grandmother, who on her deathbed said two things: "I always put out the lights before I made love" and "Never go to Chicago." And of how he did come to America, the recipient of a scholarship, crossing the country on a train. When he got to Pittsburgh and looked out the window and saw the blast furnaces roaring, he shook the guy sitting next to him and yelled: "Hey, the city is on fire!"

Lovaas played with Noah, noting that he was aware of his surroundings and that he obviously preferred to be with me more than with anyone else, which suggested to him that Noah wasn't so much autistic as schizophrenic. And indeed, not surprisingly, most of the evening was spent discussing Noah in general, but the business of his going on a food-deprivation program again was never brought up.

We did talk around it, though, Lovaas' main point being that everything was operant, that even suicide could be conditioned. He would not assign to the human being whatever graces may be attributed to consciousness, awareness, or imagination. I argued that the difference between a human being and an animal subject to conditioning was that the human being was more likely to be aware of the process and thus in one way or another effect the result. Finally, with the help of some *sake*, he agreed somewhat.

We also discussed the business of "fear." The Freudians always begin with the assumption that psychotic children are the victims of some terrible fear. And one must always be wary in the treatment of such children, according to the psychogenic approach, of further stirring up that fear. "But the trouble with most of these kids," according to Lovaas, "is that they don't have any fear at all. And to begin to make them function, you must forget all etiology, and implant *fear* in them. It's not that these kids fear too much; it's that they don't fear at all. If Noah, for example, was afraid of an electric shock, I'd use my stinger on him tomorrow. But at this point I don't think Noah is afraid of anything."

March 8, 1971

Noah's been out of diapers for several weeks now, so today two small but highly symbolic actions took place. I went over to the supermarket to return several unopened boxes of Pampers and Purina cat food.

March 9, 1971

Lovaas presented himself at our door last night, smiling like a young man anxious for a night out. We got into his Porsche and whizzed up and down freeways to the Sports Arena. He was excited, he had never seen a fight, and when he had mentioned that fact to me at dinner the other night I insisted that he accompany me to watch Ali's attempt to "condition" Frazier. It was a fine fight, though we both rooted for Ali and were disappointed that he lost. We drove back becalmed and went to a Spanish restaurant for some nibbles and a nightcap, two worldly men finishing out an evening on the town. But mostly we spoke of children, sick children. Lovaas is anxious to move to other areas of research, but he "just can't leave the kids." The man has a gruff exterior; he speaks English with the unfrilled directness of one speaking a second language. But beneath it all I think he is soft and loving; his actions—if not his words—are the statements of a genuine concern. After all, he's got four normal kids of his own to worry about.

March 10, 1971

I called Noah's school back home. They will take Noah back when we return east. One less worry.

But Noah himself hasn't been feeling too well these past few days. So we've been keeping him home in pajamas and a red bathrobe—in which he looks sensational. He is back in diapers too, because of his loose stomach. I hate the prospect of having him go back to diapers for even a single day. But Foumi, in her infinite wisdom, assures me it's all right.

Last night I was play-talking with Karl. Knowing his fascination with dinosaurs, I began to talk of a bald-headed dinosaur known as Baldosaurus. He was also the only dinosaur who wore glasses. And whereas some of the other dinosaurs were meat-eaters, and others were plant-eaters, Baldosaurus was the only dinosaur who was an ice-cream-eater. And on and on I went. Until finally I said: "Do you know who Baldosaurus was married to?" "Sure," said Karl. "Hairysaurus."

The only game Noah can play is to lean on one with clinging inexpressive affection. But he has begun to kiss, pressing his lips, without moving them, against one's face.

March 13, 1971

Mrs. Harris told me that she heard Noah speak in class. He turned to the boy next to him and softly said: "Bobby."

March 15, 1971

Foumi and I had another talk last night about how to deal with Noah in the long run. I think the simplest way for us to try to beat the rap is by making a lot of money and imperially hiring someone to bear the brunt of him. But Foumi is firmly against colonialism—in any manner, shape, or form.

March 16, 1971

We watched Noah at school over a closed-circuit TV. Mrs. Harris conducts the class as if it were an ordinary class, so the whole process was like watching the patient construction and perpetual reconstruction of a sand castle that keeps slipping and falling apart. And the hours stretched out in slow motion. For example, the opening ceremonies of the class day—the announcement of the day of the week, the date of the month, roll call, the pledge to the flag, the anthem, and a game song—took most of the morning.

Mrs. Harris thinks Noah should be treated like a two-year-old, a very slow two-year-old with a very low energy threshold, and she constantly talks to him as such. We'll try to do the same.

Noah also will begin a new regime at home. The accent will be on daily life, and the UCLA therapists will come to our house. Foumi and I will be instructed in how to get him through operant conditioning to do a little more for himself—eating, dressing, brushing teeth, toilet. Foumi will also learn how to teach him to play with toys; I will work with him on speech. We'll treat him gently but try constantly to direct him toward participating more and more in activities. It will be a lot of extra work for both of us, but work well worth doing.

We took Karl to Disneyland again while Noah was at school. And there was something different about devoting a day to just Karl alone, in having a small ordinary family unit. There were those brief moments when I would get the idea of what our lives would have been like without Noah. And Karl took advantage of having stage center all day by playing the prima donna—a role we don't allow him to indulge in often enough.

In this home-care program, somehow the UCLA kids seem to expect us to devote days and nights to Noah, to ignore our lives to the point of self-sacrifice. For example, we're not supposed to leave Noah alone for a second. But that's impossible.

But Noah is funny. I can ask him to pull down his pants. He does so slowly, after many takes. Next: pull down your underwear. He pulls up his pants. No. Pull *down* your pants. He pulls down his pants again. Now pull down your underwear. He pulls up his pants once more. And there is such an expression of sweet and deep confusion on his face, I want to hug him and bust him one at the same time. But he's trying. And inch by inch he's making progress.

We still carry on with the vitamins. Each day one of us dutifully mixes up with mortar and pestle a mash of Niacinimide, Inostol, pathothonic acid, Pyroxidine, Deanor, ascorbic acid, B-1, B-12, and B-15, with which Noah's daily supply of orange juice is spiked.

The therapists keep coming to our house, to teach us how to cope with ongoing situations. For example, this afternoon I watched as Meredith showed Foumi how to condition Noah in the using of a napkin. She placed a napkin in his hand, put one in her own, and said "Do this" as she wiped her face. Each time that Noah did this, he was rewarded with a Frito.

Yesterday when Laura was over, she finally explained to me some of the results of her experiments, such as the spaghetti-tangle-wired machine which used to reward Noah with a Frito whenever he responded to a sound or sight stimuli. Autistic children, she's come to conclude, can respond to only one sense, whereas most normal learning requires at least two senses, audio and visual. For example, if you say to an autistic child, "This is John," and point to the person named John, the autistic child will either hear you say "This is John" or see you point to the person named John. But not both. Which, of course, makes learning hard.

With all of the heavy learning artillery we're firing at Noah, I still feel resigned to his eventual loss. I mean, someday we'll have to give him up to some sort of institution. I spoke to Lovaas informally the other day and on the basis of his experience he all but agreed, holding out little hope in the long run. So what are we knocking ourselve out for?

Because I don't think we have any other viable alternative at the moment. That's why. I don't see what institution we could trust to take care of Noah. At the same time, we have to be careful not to use Noah as an excuse for whatever mess—or messes—we tend to make of our lives. When we get home I have to be sure Foumi gets time to paint each day, to exercise in even the smallest way her enormous talents, to at least break up her never-ending latrine details.

The UCLA kids, Laura and Meredith and Tom, keep coming daily, and last night Alys Harris was over for dinner. She is that rarity, someone who is sincere in her work and sure of her prowess at the same time—a good teacher. We learned much from her and got confused a little in so doing. She thinks Noah isn't quite autistic but that he's emotionally disturbed. She counsels that we must move along slowly with him, not push too hard. Most important, we must forget all the things he couldn't do or once could do. Instead, we must teach him slowly, patiently, to do whatever he can presently do. She reminded us of how much he has progressed in the past few months: he now urinates standing up; he rarely has more than one accident a day; he holds a pencil, he paints, he plays with puzzles, he no longer is completely uninterested in toys. In short, we should treat him not as if he were inevitably doomed but as if he were immediately educable. Indeed, the great lesson we've learned out here—from Dr. Lovaas and from Alys Harris—is that Noah can be taught more easily than he can be categorized.

Noah kept coming out of his crib to inspect Alys Harris. Seeing her in the unusual environment of his own home really seemed to throw him. Karl, on the other hand, was unusually subdued and quiet. There was a teacher in the house—even if it wasn't his teacher—and so he put on his best school manners.

Every parent must face the ultimate *loss* of a child—
sooner or later. We've just had to face it sooner. But now
that we're resigned to it, we can accept it. And now that
we know Noah can be trained, I think we can manage to
hold on and hang in a little longer than we previously anticipated. Oh, how I hope so.

The first sound is the hardest sound. Noah has begun to
grunt back an "ah" from me on cue. His sound is primitive, it comes from the throat, like one straining to defecate
or vomit. But I esteem it as important a breakthrough as
the "wah" of Helen Keller, the *"eau"* of *The Wild Child*.
Yesterday I tried converting it into an "eat," the day before to an "oh." But it does not matter, whether he is
speaking our precise language or not, he now knows that
certain sounds will get him things he wants: food and approval.

And at school he now gets on the swing by himself,
climbs up the slide. So perhaps here in California, before
we prepare to return home, we have at last come in out of
the cold.

Meredith tried to cue Noah visually rather than with
sounds. Whenever she held up a green token, Noah was
supposed to pick up a model car. But Noah seemed to respond no more quickly to visual cues than to oral ones.
Noah can learn, but his learning process is oh so painfully
slow.

In the early evening I took Noah to a playground in Santa Monica. He interested himself in the sand pile for a while. But when I gave him free rein, he just headed off into the mowed green yonder of the rolling lawns. And if I had not chased after him, I know he would have never come back.

Laura has told me that she is convinced that Noah is "autistic" in the traditional sense because she has noticed that when he hurts himself he does not come crying to his parents for help or solace. But I have noticed that when I have hurt him by whacking him for something—as when he grabbed food from my plate tonight at dinner —he will come to me, crying out for comfort. Or perhaps justice.

April 4, 1971

It's difficult to mold Noah's "ah." I'm trying to use "eat" as a cue for the "ah" response which I reinforce. At the same time, I start teaching him the "O" sound. I'm doing so by trying to get him to imitate my lip formation. If his lips are in the right position when he makes his "ah" sound, it will come out "O"—and his phonetic vocabulary will be doubled.

April 5, 1971

Last night I was sick, headachy, had a sore throat. And in the throes of incipient hypochondria I began to wonder what would happen to Noah if Foumi or I were to die. And the thoughts in my head began to bang against that old institutional wall.

We drove down to San Diego to see Dr. Bernard Rimland, who perhaps has done more for the cause of autistic children in America than any other single person. Rimland, an experimental psychologist in the employ of the U.S. Navy, is the head of the Institute for Child Behavior Research and the founding father of the National Society for Austistic Children. He is the father of a fifteen-year-old autistic son, Mark.

It was Mark who answered the door when we arrived at the Rimland home, a sweet-faced boy whom one could see would never quite be a man. Mark was good-mannered, had all the social graces, and along with his thirteen-year-old sister and seven-year-old brother tried to entertain Karl and Noah while we talked with his parents. But Karl was shy and put on his "I want to go home" number while Noah went into his self-stim pounce and dance step.

Mrs. Rimland told us that though Mark's motor development had been normal, he was in diapers until age six and did not begin to speak until he was eight. So she spent many sleepless nights and tired days on the edge of that hysteria that an autistic child can engender in his parent. And Dr. Rimland said the turning point for Mark came when he learned of Lovaas and operant conditioning and began to apply those techniques to Mark. Dr. Rimland was also excited about the results achieved through the use of vitamins.

At one point in the evening we left Noah alone in the living room as we wandered into the study which houses the Institute. When we returned, there was a turd on the rug, a dropping from Noah. I did not chastise him in the least. I knew Dr. and Mrs. Rimland would understand.

And I was delighted that Noah had first pulled down his pants. Progress.

Indeed, seeing Mark, observing the ongoing family unit, we left the Rimland home feeling hope about the future.

April 8, 1971

I was talking to an old friend, an old army buddy, who is now in the movie business. "You have an automatic reality builder in Noah," he said to me. "It's easy for the rest of us out here to lose sight of who we are and what we care for."

April 9, 1971

Noah had one of his classic days—frequent toilet accidents, constant shrieks, and then a beaut of a night. I don't think he ever closed his eyes—or allowed us to. So this morning found Foumi going to the closet, packing a suitcase: "I can't go on. My hair is turning white, my eyes can't focus, I'm losing my voice, I'm not painting. I feel I'm simply throwing my life away because of this crazy kid." All I could do was agree. There is no solving the problem, there is only the deferring of it. Meanwhile, I guess I have to share more of the unpleasant labors.

April 10, 1971

I look at the other kids at Noah's school, kids older than he is, kids who seem to have come a long way. And the sad thing is, they're no bargains either. So I begin to wonder: is it worth all the effort? The books I will not write, the paintings Foumi will not paint, the parental attention Karl will never get? And the answer is obvious. Of course, it is easy to sentimentalize: how having a Noah gives meaning and definition to one's life. How people without Noahs are constantly searching for humanistic dedications. How a Noah teaches one the values of all the old verities. Bullshit! Without Noah we'd be freer to explore the boundaries of our own lives instead of constantly trying to pierce his perimeters.

April 11, 1971

There was an item in today's paper about mounting scientific belief that homosexuality is biochemically based. I showed it to Foumi, and she nodded. So they were coming around to the belief that almost all behavior has a biochemical genesis, that man can neither will nor dictate his genes—though eventually he may be able to direct them.

For Foumi and I both agree that if Noah were "normal" he would probably be homosexual. One can see it in his textures, his soft femininity. When I hug him sometimes on my bed, he evokes not only bundles of parental love from me but also a kind of pure homosexual love.

April 12, 1971

Noah removes me from the world of wars, yet at the same time enhances my understanding of Vietnams. I can easily see how a nation which so cruelly treats its own "gooks," its own second-class citizens, its own smitten children, can lack all compassion for any people or land that is foreign and alien, different and deviant.

169

April 13, 1971

I guess it's all a matter of education: we have to teach Noah and learn how to endure ourselves.

April 14, 1971

We're packing again, sending things off again, moving on again—still bearing, as the saying goes, our problem with us. But I see no other way to play it except from alternative to alternative, from shot to shot.

I'm not yet completely sold on behaviorism, but I do think operant conditioning is the right approach for Noah. For without operant conditioning we would just be waiting somehow for disjointed miracles, manna from the oral —and oracular—heavens. The idea is simply to be able to control Noah, to make him a robot, if possible, in terms of socially acceptable behavior. For if we can't control him, or get him to control himself, we'll have to let him go. In microcosm, isn't this the dilemma of modern man: how to avoid being a destructive uncontrolled spirit and still not wind up a mechanistic animal, as programmed as a robot? And I'll be damned if I know the answer.

Today Noah had his "after" TV taping at UCLA, first alone in a room, then with a quiet stranger, and finally with the stranger guiding him in play. The correlations and comparisons with the first tapings did not reveal any dramatic improvements. But to my naked eye and rangy memory he still seems to have come a long way.

And last night we hosted a jolly party at a Chinese restaurant for Lovaas and his crew. It was just a token way of our saying thank you for all the work they've done with Noah—and us.

Last packing day. I spoke to Lovaas again. He was pessimistic, reminded me that only one in twenty autistics really make it out of their condition. But Alys Harris, on the other hand, was enthusiastic about Noah's prospects. She mentioned how aware he had become of the other children, how his behavior was more social in the sandbox, how he had filled out physically and now enjoyed a hearty appetite. And, most important, she said: "Noah wants to learn, and is proud of himself when he learns."

I feel a little sad and confused about leaving California. I'm not sure our facilities back home may be the most fruitful for Noah. Nor am I sure that I would like to stay in California, that my muted but mythic destiny lies here. But I do know that I return east with a less guilt-prone heart.

Home again. We got in from the airport at almost eleven o'clock last Friday night and found a WELCOME HOME sign, a basically stocked refrigerator, and some deliciously baked health-food cookies from the neighbors. After the anonymous, centerless sprawl of Los Angeles, living where one never really felt one had neighbors, it was good to be back amid the vestiges of an old American town spirit. Here our neighbors view us as we view them —with liking and a sense of responsibility.

And the kids have been happy too, rediscovering their home, prancing about it. Karl marvels at each old toy discovered anew, Noah enjoys the delights of steps leading to a second story again. Noah also seems to like our yard.

When he went outside, the first thing he did was go to the swing hanging from our deck—something he was never interested in before. And then he began to explore our frontier-like hilly backyard, a sharp contrast to the flat, neatly tailored gardens of Los Angeles.

Yesterday, Monday, still accustomed to California time, we overslept. But by midmorning I finally got Noah off to his school, where he was warmly welcomed. One of his classmates, the little girl with the Downs syndrome, even recognized him, calling out: "Noah." He didn't react to it in any noticeable way.

By the time I got Karl to his school, his class was recessing. One girl on a swing spotted him and shouted: "Karl." Then the rest of the children came running, gathering about him. And I left him there, the smiling center of attention, seeming very glad to be home.

April 21, 1971

I love the promises of home, the hints of spring, the joys of seeing another season bloom—something we missed in Los Angeles. For the first time our lilac bush is going to flower, the crocuses are peeking through, the mimosa is just beginning to bud, the days are warm, though a refreshing wind blows. And as I look out my window, instead of seeing a blanket of smog I see the river and its other bank several miles away.

But in the midst of our homecoming euphoria we must not lose sight of all that we've gained in California. Noah is out of diapers. He can be pushed and prodded further along the developmental trail than we had previously imagined. If he's far behind others, he's still ahead of himself as he's been. And, most important, we now have more confidence in our ability to cope with him—something we must never again let anybody or any ideology take away from us.

April 23, 1971

Last night I went to a meeting of the board at Noah's school. At the end of the meeting I was talking to the board president when an elderly man approached. "How's it going, Jim?" the president asked. Jim replied: "I miss him something awful." The president explained to me: "Jim's wife died during the winter. And Jim soon found he couldn't take care of his twenty-three-year-old son anymore and had to put him away." "The house," Jim went on saying, "feels awful empty."

April 24, 1971

Karl was ready early. So instead of driving him to the bus stop this morning, I took him all the way to school. He was happy to beat the bus. "I'll be the first from Bus 13," he said proudly as he left the car.

When I returned home I found Noah rolling adamantly on the floor. He would not go upstairs, he would not allow Foumi to begin the process of dressing him. After I force-dressed him, it was evident that he was angry with me, annoyed to the point of tantrum at the fact that I had left the house, jealous that I had gone off for a long period of time without him—and with Karl. Noah has normal sibling feelings, damnit, that we can't afford to indulge because his expressions of them are abnormal in both tone and degree.

Karl is in the playroom, drawing with his crayons; Noah sits in his sandbox, and a neighbor's teen-age daughter who has taken the lyrical step from gawkiness to maturity during our absence, shows him how to fill a pail and empty it. The trees are budding, and soon our view of the river will be filled in by clusters of green, and our grass will be growing wildly, the signs of life, even uncontrollable life, rampant. And I remind myself that I must relearn the lesson of patience with Noah. In the last few sessions I've had with him, I've expected too much. I should be satisfied with less, appreciative of the fact that he has to keep moving in order to stand still. And I should rejoice more in seeing him play with toys placed before him. He can turn his music box, pull his xylophonic teddy, push a shape into a puzzle box.

Noah and the septuagenarian taxi man who drives him home from his school have always had something special going between them. And they seem to have picked up just where they left off. They are both still all smiles whenever Noah gets out of his cab. I asked him today if he thinks Noah remembers him. "Of course," he said, with the surety of the old that is arrogance in others. "How could he forget me? I'm his friend." He also added that he thinks Noah has changed much for the better.

I still get frustrated by Noah's utter dumbness. When one makes a request of him, he does what he knows rather than what you ask. If I ask him, for example, to put his finger in his mouth to thus shape his lips so that the sound

"O" can emerge from him, he claps his hands or grunts an "uh," a sound or gesture that has earned him approval in the past.

Each day Foumi and I discharge our therapy chores, our operant-conditioning chores. Foumi tries to teach him to play: to catch a ball, to select an object, to thread plastic beads. I work on speech, at this point concentrating on getting him to repeat the sound of "O," rewarding him with a smidgen of Frito or a sliver of potato chip when he does so, and withdrawing the reward when he fails to do so. Both the play therapy and the speech therapy go slowly.

Yesterday I told Foumi I have little faith in any therapy—vitamins or operant conditioning or anything. She said, "Then why don't we just put him in an institution?" And I couldn't think of an answer. So I pulverized the vitamins more thoroughly and worked that much harder with Noah today.

Today's thought: Freud performed the old trick of simple inversion, and treated it as if it were significant insight. He looked at children as if they were adults, and adults as if they were children.

Another thought: neuroses are bad habits, psychoses bad genes.

A closeout thought: anyone who uses words like "we" or "us" is attempting to generalize some personal and idiosyncratic ideology into an all-pervasive moral point of view. *We* should never trust them.

May 3, 1971

Oh, the feeling tonight when I walked into the house and saw Karl and Noah and Foumi as glad to see me as I was to see them after a day away. Sometimes I think I spend too much time with my family to truly appreciate them.

May 5, 1971

I went to see a noted dog trainer last night, hoping to learn about his training and conditioning techniques. Perhaps some of them could apply to Noah, I thought. But he wasn't very helpful, was entirely too secretive. It's a joke. I'll even look to dog trainers for a sign, the symbol of an eventual cure, for Noah.

Noah still wets himself during the day, his crib at night, and has tantrums when he does not get what he wants, when we don't meet his desires. But perhaps, just like any normal child his age, in his own way he's testing authority.

May 6, 1971

There was a meeting of the parents of the kids in Noah's class. The teacher, whom I have come to respect more and more, outlined the schedule of a class day. It was the usual one: individual instruction, group activity, circle time, outdoor play. The last is Noah's favorite. Sometimes he even doesn't want to go indoors when I bring him to school. If only we could have Los Angeles weather here without the smog.

Noah hates to be put through his learning paces, rebels so when I begin them. But so, too, I notice, does Karl. And if I think back hard enough, I can recall how much I hated to do homework.

I have to adopt a tough line with Noah, though, not allowing his mood to dominate our session. And in spite of his protesting tears, recently it is obvious that his attention span is lengthening. Once we get the crying over with—as with Karl—he does get down to work.

After our session today I gave him a lollipop, a red one, the only flavor he'll accept. I so enjoy watching him lick-drool it, in every child's gooey way, his face becoming a glazed slurp of sugary delight.

Noah goes through stages, has his periods. Foumi says he's much easier to take care of these days again. He listens more, he observes more. And they say the same thing in school. Perhaps we'll be able to manage him longer than we had anticipated.

What do I dream of now? Beautiful women? Far-off travel? Exotic friends? Princely wealth? No. None of these things. I simply dream continually of a normal Noah.

And there are hints to feed the dream. Last night, he suddenly sat beside me, on the edge of the couch, and like any father and son—even if briefly—we were watching a TV baseball game together.

We went to Connecticut, and again were impressed with the special day school in New Haven that goes from 9:30 A.M. to 4:30 P.M., Monday to Saturday, fifty-two weeks a year. Noah is still too young for the school, but it's something we have to think about in the long run—which for us means in a year or two.

Noah has his "accidents." But his box score is improving tremendously: he's slept through the night without wetting himself for six of the last seven nights. And we've also been able to catch most of his b.m.'s lately.

I spoke too soon. Last night Noah awoke with a bundle in his pants. But what the hell, he's entitled to his errors. And he is happy and alert lately. And so, too, of course, are we.

Foumi also observed Noah in school today and was quite pleased with what she saw. He was trying to learn, and they were trying to teach him. Which is all we can ask of him and of any educational—or treatment—setup.

I appreciated the new Noah this morning. We had a late night, but he slept through again, not wetting himself. And after breakfast he went to the john on cue. So he has become much easier to take care of. The box score for the toilet week ending today, for example, was no daytime accidents, one wake-up wet, and one wake-up soiled. And that record is just as mythic to me as Babe Ruth's. Foumi points out that not only is that a psychological relief, but the lifting of a physical burden as well. No more time-consuming, energy-draining "special" loads for the washing machine each day.

Some friends dropped in with a friend of theirs, a social worker at the hospital where Noah was first examined by a psychologist-psychiatrist team way back when. The hospital has a day-care treatment school and at the time Noah was examined we were led to believe that eventually he would be accepted there. Now the social worker tells us, "socially" and "off the record," that Noah was the victim of an administration hassle. The psychologist wanted Noah to be admitted to the school, but the administration rejected her recommendation because the hospital receives more money from the state for the treatment of a physically handicapped child than for an autistic one.

It's too far back to be bitter about. I am glad when any sick child, not only mine, finds treatment. At the same time, I can't help but resent the fact that children like Noah are at the bottom of state-aid troughs, bumped by hospitals to make room for higher-revenue-producing sick children.

It's all so *sick* anyway—part of the psychogenic bind —and blind. Because every autistic child, I realize now, is in one way or another neurologically impaired—or brain-damaged. The rest is semantic niceties.

I spoke on the telephone with the mother of an eleven-year-old autistic boy. She seems to have done everything we've tried to do, been everywhere we've been. Her son too took his first steps toward toilet training because of a talented teacher. "Every activity, with our children, even the simplest one," she told me, "has to be a taught one." And we discussed what happens to "our children" when they become older. She mentioned some parents who purposely had other children just so there would be somebody to look after their "autistic one" after they died. "Still," she said, "you have to remember things are getting better for 'our children.' They're better now than they were five years ago. And let's hope they'll be that much better five years from now." But she was not that optimistic about "our children" in the long run. Very few ever get so they can support themselves, take care of themselves by way of being able to make the simplest everyday decisions. Most of us, this mother and I finally agreed, for all of our hopes and dreams, are still fattening up our children for the inevitable institutional kill. For that is the setting they seemed destined for, an institutional one. "Like," I added compensatingly, "all the other members of the nuclear family."

A day with Noah: on the typical schoolday, Foumi, Karl, and I get up at about 7:50. We then breakfast together separately from Noah. Karl is entitled to begin a day as the center of attention, as the star attraction. Second, once Noah sees bread or toast on the table, it is impossible to get him to eat or drink anything else. So we try to get Karl, who has an 8:38 bus to catch, on his way before dealing with Noah. Meanwhile, Noah, awakened by the alarm, is pouncing about on his bed. Once breakfast is over, I take him to the bathroom and try to get him to take care of his toilet needs, wash him if he's wetted during the night, and change him. Noah then comes downstairs and is greeted by juice, eggs, fruit, and toast, in that order. These days he eats well. While he is at breakfast, Foumi is preparing his lunch—a piece of fruit, peeled and placed in a plastic container; some meat; salad greens; and a thermos of either juice or chocolate milk, laced with his vitamins. At 9:10 I manage to get him out of the house, and we're at his school by about 9:15.

At school he removes his jacket or coat and hangs it in his cubby and pushes his little chair toward his place at the table he shares with his classmates, a puzzle or a toy usually awaiting him there. From then on his class has the usual kindergarten routine: circle, songs, sandbox, block corner, outdoor play, lunch, rest—but not in quite that order. A teacher and a teacher's aide keep the children busy—except during the rest period—until 1:30. Then they prepare for the end of the schoolday.

Noah is usually home by two o'clock, his old crony, the septuagenarian cab driver, delivering him in his stationwagon taxi. He then plays in our yard, making forays to the swing, the sandbox, but most often running the pebbles of our rock garden through his fingers repeatedly, as if he were looking for some rare gem among them. Foumi next prevails upon him to enter the house, where he is taken to the bathroom, offered some refreshment, and set to work on his therapies. Foumi tries to teach him how to play with toys, how to crawl à-la-patterning, how to distinguish the letter *A* from the letter *O*—all with the rewards and the prods of operant conditioning. She does so until Karl comes home at 3:30 and she has to supervise his reading and homework.

At 4:30 I usually arrive on the scene. And although I don't have a very good teaching personality, I sit down with Noah for a little speech work. It is still slow and frustrating, but I stay with it as long as we both seem productive.

By this time Karl is outside playing, Foumi is busy preparing dinner, and I, unfortunately, sometimes have a few phone calls to return. Left alone for even a moment, Noah is quick to resume one of his self-stim nonactivities—lying down on the couch, pouncing about the room, bouncing in his crib upstairs. And one of us duly admonishes and chastises him for it with a, "No. Stop it."

Since we are a rice-eating family, at dinner we do with rice as we did with bread at breakfast, withhold it until Noah has eaten his fill of the protein course. Then we all sit down and join him. Afterward, I generally play with Karl, always, though, looking over at Noah from time to time, playing with his Slinky or draped over a chair, until he seems to indicate that he might be in the market for a bowel movement. There are no sure signs, only vague indications—a move toward the stairs, a withdrawal into a corner, a downward tug at his pants. I then take him to the bathroom. We're successful about half of the time. The rest is clean-up time.

Next comes his bath, a change into p.j.'s, a decent wait, a final urination. And then bed. He climbs into his crib in a ritualistic sort of a way, first walking around it, pushing the chair that is his step away from it, ducking through the chair frame from the inside, and finally climbing up and in. We still keep him in a crib because it means smaller sheets to clean and has a waterproof mattress. The chances that he will wet during the night keep diminishing but are still present.

Lately, he sleeps the night through—without bed-wetting—about 75 percent of the time. We're greatly appreciative of the change.

Gradually, I would say, we tend to ignore Noah more and more as the afternoon wears on. He drains a great deal of energy without recharging us as battery sources by means of the simple gestures of reciprocity—what the psychologists call "feedback." Noah appreciates affection, is all cuddly, but he never seems to initiate a hug or impulsively lavish a kiss. Foumi claims he sometimes comes over to her and presses his lips against hers. And at times he does the same thing to me. But I'm convinced he's considering more a bite than a kiss on those occasions—and sometimes I have the tooth nibble marks to prove it.

May 27, 1971

The other day Karl found the imprint of a fossil in our yard. We were all excited. And we told him to take it to school and show it to his teacher. His regular teacher was absent that day, the substitute was unimpressed, and he came home with the rock damaged. "It isn't worth anything." He threw it on the floor. "That's what the other kids said." The cruelty of both students and a school system! I explained to Karl that things can have a more important value than a monetary one—a scientific one. And I brought him and the stone over to a local amateur archaeologist, who examined the rock and said that it came from the Devonian period of the Paleozoic age—some three to four hundred million years ago; that it was not a rock indigenous to this immediate area; and that it probably arrived here via the Wisconsin spill, a glacial slide of antiquity, or more recently via a contractor's fill. In any case, Karl listened most attentively, and at last was properly impressed with the value and importance of his backyard discovery.

May 28, 1971

This morning at breakfast one of Noah's favorite foods was placed before him. And he was not allowed to partake of it until he uttered the magic word. And he finally did so: "Bagel," he shrieked, clear as a bell.

May 29, 1971

Foumi and I, after much discussion, have laid down two basic ground rules about Noah. 1: We will go only to places we want to go to anyway in order to find better treatment for him. 2: We will not alter our lives, or life style, because of him alone; it is too great a load to place on his slender and tender person.

May 30, 1971

At five o'clock this morning a woman was at the door ringing the bell and calling up to our bedroom window: "Get out! The firemen want you out. The house behind you is on fire." Foumi was up first, opening the window, talking to the woman below. And then I was looking out a back window, seeing a neighbor's house, less than one hundred yards away, afire, great flames and sparking embers flying our way. We roused the kids, a frightened Karl, a moist Noah. We dressed them and put them into the car, preparing for a quick getaway. I began to evacuate Foumi's paintings, some of my papers. And then a neighbor from below came up with his teen-age son to help water down our roof. Soon the wind changed, and the fire seemed to be dying down, and I left Foumi and the kids and reconnoitered down and around the block, seeing the great ruin the fire had wrought, only a gutted front facade and a single corner room remaining, the rest all burning down between the two great chimneys. Fortunately, no one was in the house, the occupants being away for the holiday weekend. And as the neighboring housewives were dispensing coffee to the firemen, the mood suddenly seemed block-party-carnival against a background of sheer destruction.

I returned to our driveway and carried Karl and Noah back into the house, Noah protesting most vehemently.

Obviously he felt that he had been cheated out of a car ride he had been promised.

When I put Karl back to bed he asked me: "Does Noah think that we're all autistic?" We could both hear Noah, in the next room, still whining. I tucked in Karl's top sheet, answering: "Probably yes."

June 2, 1971

Tonight for the first time Noah, receiving lavish praise every step of the way, got into the bathtub by himself—and stayed there. Until now one of us has had to get into the tub with him. And we often wondered what would happen when he became too big for that. Hopefully, that worry may now be over.

June 9, 1971

I asked Noah at breakfast: "Do you want juice?" And he clearly replied: "I want juice." Foumi and I now feel that Noah will eventually speak again. We don't take much stock in the opinion that children who do not speak by the age of five never speak. We think there is no set rule, no s.o.p. in regard to a child like Noah. And we note that Noah seems to be aware more of our speech, of what we're saying, which has to be a prelude to any speech on his part.

June 11, 1971

Karl, while being bathed in the tub, was asking Foumi all about sex and how the seed got into the woman's stomach. Foumi told him it entered through the vagina. And he stopped his questioning there. "What'll I say when he asks the next question?" she asked me. "Stop giving him baths," I replied. "Let the kids take cold showers."

June 15, 1971

Foumi's been interviewing girls, college psychology majors and graduates, trying to find help for us during the long summer ahead. One of them, the most promising candidate, told Foumi that she had thought of going to work in an institution. But then all her friends who had gone to work in them told her what the institutions were like: most were Potemkins, facades constructed just for the visiting days of parents. Only then the children were cleaned, the facilities spic-and-spanned; otherwise, the children were neglected and the hallways and wards were nightmare alleys of filth.

June 17, 1971

I lack the magic of the teacher's art, the industry of the dedicated professional. My sessions with Noah aren't going half as well as Foumi's. She's taught him how to blow sounds out of a harmonica.

June 18, 1971

Karl's class picnic: how bourgeois the air, how springy the grass, how far from the schoolyard pavements of my own boyhood. There were hot dogs and potato chips and watermelon and cupcakes. And he was delighted that I was one of the handful of fathers there.

And afterward he brought home his gift for Father's Day, a bound folder of mimeographed compositions by each member of the class about his father. Karl's was a Proustian reverie in which he recalled thankfully the custard cones I had bought him at the local Carvel stand, a set of plastic planes I once picked up for him in a Beverly Hills toy store, and his trips to Disneyland. His first two "memories" I could scarcely recall—or even think of as memories. Which goes to show you. A parent can't implant significance into an event; the significance always lies in the eyes of the little beholder.

June 21, 1971

The picnic season continues. We went to one yesterday, and many friends whom we hadn't seen in a long time were amazed at the changes in Noah—and us. We could leave him alone, did not have to worry about his wetting himself; we could be loose. Indeed, someone remarked how wonderful it was that we could be so relaxed with a child like Noah. "That's because," said Foumi, "since California we know what to do." And she was right. As simple as that.

June 22, 1971

I still get infuriated with Karl. He wears his sneakers as if they were a totem. He's convinced they make him run faster, get him to his school bus quicker. And this morning when we were sure that he would miss the school bus because he spent so long precisely lacing the sneakers, I really yelled at him. But then he did run fast enough to catch the bus.

We saw the vitamin doctor, and he noticed a marked improvement in Noah. And whether the improvement is most attributable to the vitamins, or to operant conditioning, or to just the natural course of maturation, or to a combination of these factors, the doctor did not care. "It doesn't matter what's most responsible," he said. "What matters is that Noah is more responsive."

June 24, 1971

This morning Karl was full of anticipatory joy. I awoke to find him struggling over a note:

I CAN HAV GOLDFI-
SH

His teacher, it seems, had announced that she would give one of the six goldfish from the class bowl to whichever child had permission from his parents. I signed Karl's note. But when I picked him up at school, I discovered him tearful; he was the one child who had lost in the lottery for the goldfish. So now I have to get him a tankful of them.

Noah coming home from school was something else. He found that we had removed his crib from his room. In its place there was a mattress on the floor—just as in everyone else's room in our house. For a long time he looked for a place to plop down upon with his security blanket. And finally he settled on the mattress and napped.

So if he can sleep the way everyone else in his family does and can keep developing his good toilet habits, we're on the way. The way to where? I do not know. But wherever—it'll be an easier trip getting there.

June 25, 1971

Noah's taken to his new bed like a natural man. The crib stands now in our playroom, a relic of a finally bygone age, an heirloom about to be passed on.

June 27, 1971

Foumi was watching Karl play with Mark, a neighbor's four-year-old boy, and suddenly Karl was hitting him. "Don't hit Mark!" she shouted. "I'm not hitting Mark," Karl replied. "He won't put away the toys—I'm giving him operant conditioning."

July 1, 1971

It wasn't until after I dropped him off at his school's summer camp this morning that I realized today was Noah's birthday. Five years old. And I thought back to the hot day of his birth and wondered where the five years had gone, how quickly they all seemed to have passed—just like with any other kid.

And Noah is so funny now about going to his room and

getting into bed at sleep time. When we tell him to do so, he does so, but his evasive acts, delaying tactics—such as going to the bathroom, pulling a paper cup out of the dispenser, and holding it against the cold-water tap—are just like those of any other kid.

But now finally he and Karl are off to sleep. The house is quiet. Foumi's put a pie into the oven, and now she's at her desk writing—lately she's begun a new sideline career, having published two articles in two of Japan's leading magazines. And I've just gone to the bookcase to check on that first sentence of Tolstoy's, and come away shaking my head. "Happy families," I know, "are *not* all alike."

ABOUT THE AUTHOR

Josh Greenfeld is a novelist (*O For a Master of Magic*) and a playwright (Clandestine on the Morning Line) who frequently contributes book reviews and articles to such publications as *Life*, *Time*, *The New York Times*, *Playboy*, and *The Village Voice*.